Critical Theory: A Very Short Introduction

Very Short Introductions available now:

For more information visit our web site
www.oup.co.uk/general/vsi/

Stephen Eric Bronner

CRITICAL
THEORY

A Very Short Introduction

OXFORD
UNIVERSITY PRESS

OXFORD
UNIVERSITY PRESS

Oxford University Press, Inc., publishes works that further
Oxford University's objective of excellence
in research, scholarship, and education.

Oxford   New York
Auckland   Cape Town   Dar es Salaam   Hong Kong   Karachi
Kuala Lumpur   Madrid   Melbourne   Mexico City   Nairobi
New Delhi   Shanghai   Taipei   Toronto

With offices in
Argentina   Austria   Brazil   Chile   Czech Republic   France   Greece
Guatemala   Hungary   Italy   Japan   Poland   Portugal   Singapore
South Korea   Switzerland   Thailand   Turkey   Ukraine   Vietnam

Published by Oxford University Press, Inc.
198 Madison Avenue, New York, NY 10016

www.oup.com

Oxford is a registered trademark of Oxford University Press

Library of Congress Cataloging-in-Publication Data
Bronner, Stephen Eric, 1949–
Critical theory : a very short introduction / Stephen Eric Bronner.
p. cm.
Includes index.
ISBN 978-0-19-973007-0 (pbk.)
1. Critical theory.   I. Title.
HM480.B76 2011
301.01—dc22   2010027472

9

Printed in Great Britain
by Ashford Colour Press Ltd., Gosport, Hants.
on acid-free paper

In memory of Ernst Bloch

Contents

List of illustrations

Introduction: what is critical theory?

Philosophy has evidenced a subversive element from its inception. Plato's *Apology* tells how Socrates was condemned by the Athenian citizenry for corrupting the morals of the young and doubting the gods. There was some truth to that complaint. Socrates called conventional wisdom into question. He subjected long-standing beliefs to rational scrutiny and speculated about concerns that projected beyond the existing order. What became known as "critical theory" was built upon this legacy. The new philosophical tendency was generated between World War I and World War II, and its most important representatives would wage an unrelenting assault on the exploitation, repression, and alienation embedded within Western civilization.

Critical theory refuses to identify freedom with any institutional arrangement or fixed system of thought. It questions the hidden assumptions and purposes of competing theories and existing forms of practice. It has little use for what is known as "perennial philosophy." Critical theory insists that thought must respond to the new problems and the new possibilities for liberation that arise from changing historical circumstances. Interdisciplinary and uniquely experimental in character, deeply skeptical of tradition and all absolute claims, critical theory was always concerned not merely with how things were but how they might

1

be and should be. This ethical imperative led its primary thinkers to develop a cluster of themes and a new critical method that transformed our understanding of society.

Critical theory has many sources. Immanuel Kant identified moral autonomy as the highest value for the individual. He provided critical theory with its definition of scientific rationality, and its goal of confronting reality with the prospects of freedom. Meanwhile Hegel understood consciousness as the motor of history, thinking as linked to practical concerns, and philosophy as "its epoch comprehended in thought." Critical theorists learned to interpret the particular with an eye on the totality. The moment of freedom appeared in the demand for recognition by the enslaved and the exploited.

Both Kant and Hegel incarnated the cosmopolitan and universal assumptions deriving from the European Enlightenment of the seventeenth and eighteenth centuries. They relied upon reason to combat superstition, prejudice, cruelty, and the arbitrary exercise of institutional authority. They also speculated about the humane hopes expressed by aesthetics, the redemptive longings of religions, and new ways of thinking about the relation between theory and practice. The young Karl Marx went even farther with his utopian reflections on human emancipation.

Critical theory was conceived within the intellectual crucible of Marxism. But its leading representatives were from the start dismissive of economic determinism, the stage theory of history, and any fatalistic belief in the "inevitable" triumph of socialism. They were concerned less with what Marx called the economic "base" than the political and cultural "superstructure" of society. Their Marxism was of a different variety. They highlighted its critical method over its systematic claims, its concern with alienation and reification, its complicated relationship with the ideals of the Enlightenment, its utopian moment, its emphasis upon the role of ideology, and its commitment to resist the

2

deformation of the individual. This complex of themes constitutes the core of critical theory as it was conceived by the leading figures of "Western Marxism": Karl Korsch and Georg Lukács. These two thinkers provided the framework for the critical project that later became identified with the Institute for Social Research—or "the Frankfurt School."

Its principal members included Theodor W. Adorno, notable for his consummate knowledge of music and philosophy, who began his collaboration with the Institute in 1928, but did not become an official member until ten years later; Erich Fromm, a gifted psychologist, who started his nine-year collaboration in 1930; Herbert Marcuse, a philosopher with wide-ranging talents, who joined in 1933; Walter Benjamin, the most creative of these thinkers, who never officially was a member at all; and Jürgen Habermas, who became its leading philosopher in the aftermath of 1968 and surely the most prolific thinker associated with the Institute. Its guiding light, however, was Max Horkheimer. He brought together these extraordinary intellectuals in order to construct the interdisciplinary basis for a critical theory of society.

The Frankfurt School initially believed that its intellectual work would aid the practical prospects for revolutionary action by the proletariat. As the 1930s wore on, however, the revolution degenerated in the Soviet Union, and its prospects in Europe faded. Fascism had audaciously entered political life, and the humane hopes originally associated with modernity appeared increasingly naïve. The Frankfurt School registered this historical shift by subjecting long-standing leftist beliefs in the inherently progressive character of science and technology, popular education, and mass politics to withering interrogation.

The Enlightenment and Marxism were confronted from the standpoint of their unrealized ideals as the Frankfurt School refashioned the historical dialectic through insights gleaned from

Arthur Schopenhauer, Friedrich Nietzsche, Franz Kafka, Marcel Proust, Samuel Beckett, and the modernist heritage. Critical theory began the process of reclaiming forgotten utopian images and neglected ideals of resistance under circumstances in which the possibility for realizing them seemingly no longer existed. The result was a new form of "negative dialectics" whose popularity has only grown among contemporary academics.

The Frankfurt School had always considered establishmentarian philosophies as obstacles to bringing about a liberated society. Its members condemned the preoccupation with absolute foundations, analytic categories, and fixed criteria for verifying truth claims. They saw two main culprits: *phenomenology*, with its set ontological claims about how individuals experience existence, and *positivism*, with its demand that society be analyzed according to the criteria of the natural sciences. Both were attacked for treating society in a-historical terms and eliminating genuine subjectivity. Critical theory was intended as an alternative. It was fueled by a transformative intent and a particular concern with the culture of modern life.

Alienation and reification are the two ideas most commonly associated with critical theory. The former is usually identified with the psychological effects of exploitation and the division of labor, and the latter with how people are treated instrumentally, as "things," through concepts that have been ripped from their historical context. Pioneering studies of alienation and reification had already been undertaken by Western Marxists during the 1920s, but the Frankfurt School provided a unique sense of how these complex categories impacted upon individuals in advanced industrial society.

They investigated the ways in which thinking was being reduced to mechanical notions of what is operative and profitable, ethical reflection was tending to vanish, and aesthetic enjoyment was becoming more standardized. Critical theorists noted with alarm how interpreting modern society was becoming ever more difficult. Alienation and reification were thus analyzed in terms of how they imperiled the exercise of subjectivity, robbed the world of meaning and purpose, and turned the individual into a cog in the machine.

Auschwitz was seen as incarnating the most radical implications of alienation and reification. It was the watershed event that shattered optimistic assumptions about progress even more radically than the Lisbon earthquake did during the eighteenth century. With images of the Nazi concentration camps still fresh, Hiroshima and Nagasaki destroyed, new reports emerging about the Soviet Gulag, and McCarthyism on the rise in the United States, it appeared to the Frankfurt School as if Western civilization had generated not human development but an unparalleled barbarism. They knew that something more was required from radical thought than the usual stale critique of capitalism.

A bureaucratically administered mass society was apparently integrating all forms of resistance, obliterating genuine individuality, and generating personality structures with authoritarian predilections. Conformity was undermining autonomy. If capitalist development is connected with standardization and reification, then progress actually constitutes a form of regression. Illusions associated with the Enlightenment, uncritically accepted on the Left, thus required reexamination and modernity itself invited critique.

All members of the Frankfurt School agreed on the need for increased education to counteract authoritarian trends. But it remained unclear how effective such education might prove to be in a totally administered society. A new "culture industry"— arguably the most famous concept associated with critical theory—was constantly striving to lower the lowest common denominator in order to maximize sales. Authentic individual experience and class consciousness were being threatened by the consumerism of advanced capitalism. All this led Horkheimer, Adorno, and Marcuse to claim that the extent to which a work becomes popular—regardless of its political message—is the extent to which its radical impulse will be integrated into the system. These thinkers became champions of an experimental modernist art and, in the charged climate of the postwar period, an "Aesopian" form of convoluted writing that shielded their radical beliefs. Nevertheless, the esoteric and indirect style of critical theory only increased its appeal among radical intellectuals involved in the uprisings of the 1960s.

Critical theory always had an anticipatory character. Its advocates projected the transformation of everyday life and individual experience. The Frankfurt School not only contested

1. Radical intellectuals among the student movement of the 1960s were deeply influenced by critical theory and the Frankfurt School.

establishmentarian views of history, but projected a radical alternative. European radicals applied its ideas to reconfiguring the family, sexuality, and education. They sought to bring about a new utopian sensibility devoid of cruelty and competition. But the Frankfurt School split over the movements connected with the 1960s. Adorno and Horkheimer were skeptical. They questioned the counter-culture and the assault on tradition, the sporadic violence and the anti-intellectualism, as well as the comfort radical activists supposedly gave to the enemies of democracy. They identified the mass movements of the 1960s with those of the interwar period, and they associated utopian thinking with totalitarianism.

Genuine resistance now seemed to call for highlighting the negative moment within the critical tradition. Especially Adorno argued that the point was no longer one of merely refusing to identify freedom with any system, or collectivity, but rather of conceptualizing the "non-identity" (and heightening the tension) between the individual and society. Concern with organized resistance and institutional politics fell by the wayside in favor of an aesthetic-philosophical form of critique or, in the case of Horkheimer, a quasi-religious "longing for the totally other." The Frankfurt School still employed the method inherited from Hegel and Marx. Its most politically conservative members still viewed subjectivity as enmeshed within what it resisted: the commodity form, mass culture, and the bureaucratic society. But they cast new suspicions on universal claims, philosophical foundations, and the fixed narrative.

"Negative dialectics" anticipated many concerns associated with postmodernism and poststructuralism. So much so, in fact, that they are now often treated as expressions of critical theory. Deconstructive or poststructuralist approaches invaded the most prestigious journals and disciplines ranging from anthropology and film to religion, linguistics, and political science. They generated new insights on race and gender as well as the postcolonial world. In the process, however, critical theory lost its ability to offer an integrated critique of society, conceptualize a meaningful politics, and project new ideals of liberation. Textual exegesis, cultural preoccupations, and metaphysical disputations increasingly turned critical theory into a victim of its own success. The result has been an enduring identity crisis.

Critical theorists today must look backward in order to move forward. The Frankfurt School has enriched our understanding of the family, sexual repression, pedagogy, genocide, entertainment, literary analysis, and a host of other issues. But the critical tradition also has something to teach about the imbalances of power that mark the economy, the state, the public sphere, law, and global life. Even those thinkers who were most critical of the Enlightenment offer important grounds for a reasoned defense of it. The same holds true for liberalism and socialism. Clarifying conditions of oppression, opening avenues of resistance, and refashioning liberating ideals is still the province of critical theory. New *political* perspectives are required to accentuate the transformative prospects for change within a new global society. It is now a matter of subjecting the established forms of critical theory to the critical method. And that is as it should be. Only in this way is it possible to remain true to the original spirit of the critical enterprise.

Chapter 1
The Frankfurt School

[handwritten annotations: "ISR 9 / 1st Marxist – by Weil / labor movement." and "Background"]

The Institute for Social Research was founded in 1923. Growing out of a Marxist study group, which sought to deal with the practical problems facing the labor movement in the aftermath of the Russian Revolution, this first Marxist think tank was funded by Hermann Weil. He was an enlightened businessman, who made his fortune on the grain market in Argentina. The money was given at the urging of his son, Felix, who considered himself a "salon Bolshevik."

[handwritten annotation: "B1 of emerging imperialism but fade."]

Felix Weil's close friends included Kurt Albert Gerlach. A social democrat and an economist, he would have become the first director of the Institute. Unfortunately, however, Gerlach died of diabetes. Carl Grünberg thus took over instead. He founded the first official publication of the Institute, the Archive for the History of Socialism and the Labor Movement, which published a number of significant works including Korsch's *Marxism and Philosophy* (1923). Grünberg was joined by Henryk Grossmann, Friedrich Pollock, Fritz Sternberg, and Karl August Wittfogel. All of them were communists. They were still nostalgic for the democratic workers' councils of 1918–1921, and they envisioned a German Soviet Republic. Their intellectual efforts offer a rich variety of views on capitalist breakdown, the new role of the state, and imperialism. But this group would fade into the background,

[handwritten annotation in non-Latin script]

2. **Three leading figures of the Frankfurt School: Max Horkheimer (*left*), Theodor W. Adorno (*right*), and Jürgen Habermas (*rear*). This is the only photo of them together.**

and the general orientation of the Institute would change in 1930. That was the year in which Max Horkheimer brought together the new inner circle for what would become known as the Frankfurt School.

The inner circle

Horkheimer was born near Stuttgart into the family of a wealthy Jewish businessman. His early school years were undistinguished, and he left high school to work as an apprentice in his father's textile factory. In 1911, however, he made the acquaintance of Friedrich Pollock, who introduced him to philosophy and the social sciences, and who remained a life-long friend. Horkheimer finished high school after World War I. He flirted with communism, studied a variety of subjects at the University of

Frankfurt, and ultimately wrote a dissertation on Kant's *Critique of Judgment* (1790).

Horkheimer published very little prior to assuming his position as director. That changed following the triumph of Hitler in 1933 when he was busily attempting to relocate the Institute from Frankfurt first to Geneva, then to Paris, and finally to Columbia University in New York City. His essays of the 1930s concentrated on distinguishing critical theory from its philosophical competitors and demonstrating how liberal capitalism had betrayed its original promise by creating the psychological, racial, and political foundations of totalitarianism. Other works dealing with mass culture, instrumental rationality, and the authoritarian state paved the way for Adorno and Horkheimer's classic *Dialectic of Enlightenment* (1947). Horkheimer's thinking surely changed over the years. Nevertheless, he always retained his preoccupation with the impact of suffering and the liberating possibilities of individual experience.

Horkheimer also remained a champion of interdisciplinary research. Under his leadership, the Frankfurt School attempted to bridge the gap between normative theory and empirical work. His inaugural lecture of 1930 stressed that goal and, even while in exile, Horkheimer edited a multivolume interdisciplinary research project, Studies in Prejudice, for the American Jewish Committee. It included *Rehearsal for Destruction* (1949) by Paul Massing, which brilliantly analyzed the social origins of anti-Semitism in Imperial Germany; *Prophets of Deceit: A Study of the Techniques of the American Agitator* (1950) by Leo Lowenthal and Norbert Gutermann; and the classic *The Authoritarian Personality* (1950) by Theodor W. Adorno and a host of researchers.

Horkheimer's radicalism was inflamed by the Russian Revolution and the German Spartacus Revolt of 1919. But Stalin's purges and the emergence of a terror apparatus took their toll. Horkheimer ultimately broke not just with communism but with Marxism as well. His politics had shifted to the Right even before he brought the Institute back to Germany and served as Rector of the University of Frankfurt from 1951 to 1953. Horkheimer wound up opposing the anti-imperialist struggle in Algeria, supporting the Vietnam War, and denouncing the revolts associated with 1968.

At this point, his concern with the negation of misery took a new turn. Looking back to the Old Testament, which prohibited depicting the divine, he came to believe that preserving the idea of resistance was now possible only through the all encompassing negation of reality and the longing for emancipation. The sacred—or, better, the otherworldly—became the vantage point for confronting the profane. He took the critique of Enlightenment to its farthest extreme. Friends noted a growing flirtation with Catholicism. All links between theory and practice were sundered. Critical theory was already imperiled when Max Horkheimer died at the age of seventy-eight.

Erich Fromm was one of Horkheimer's closest friends from the early days. Fromm's specialty was psychology, but he was also deeply versed in theological matters. In fact, the psychoanalytic institute in Berlin that he established with his first wife, Frieda Reichmann, was dubbed the "Torah-peutikum." Fromm was a prolific writer and intellectually daring: he was among the very first to link the thought of Sigmund Freud with that of Marx. Today, however, Fromm is not taken very seriously. He is usually remembered for what his more academic critics considered "how to" books like *The Art of Loving* (1956)—that offered a responsible alternative to the way love is presented by mass culture; "feel good" works like *The Heart of Man* (1964)—that provided a counterweight to cynical assaults on Western culture; and supposedly superficial studies about international affairs like *May Man Prevail* (1961)—that sensibly called for the elimination of nuclear weapons and a tempering of the cold war spirit. Fromm's

Escape from Freedom (1941) is remembered for its penetrating analysis of totalitarianism. His grant inquiry into *The Anatomy of Human Destructiveness* (1973), however, has been unjustly forgotten.

Fromm grew up in an Orthodox Jewish family; he was instructed as a child by learned rabbis like Nehemiah Nobel and especially Salman Baruch Rabinkow. His dissertation was *The Jewish Law: Toward a Sociology of the Jewish Diaspora* (1922), and his earliest works treated religious themes: *The Sabbath* (1927) and, with a Marxian twist, *The Dogma of Christ* (1930). His interest in the psychological appeal and ethical impulse provided by religion never fully disappeared, in spite of the atheism he adopted during the 1920s, and he struck a popular chord with his humanistic reinterpretation of the Old Testament in *You Shall be as Gods* (1967). Fromm's attempt to develop a "materialist psychology" reflected the original commitment of critical theory to an all-embracing social transformation. Emphasis upon the practical character of psychoanalysis, its connection with resisting repression and fostering humanistic values, would mark his career.

Fromm helped found the Mexican Psychoanalytic Association in 1962, and he became one of the most influential figures in the development of psychoanalysis in Latin America. A staunch opponent of the Vietnam War and American imperialism, a supporter of countless progressive causes, Fromm advocated a non-bureaucratic and participatory form of "communitarian socialism." He was also unquestionably the finest stylist and the most lucid writer produced by the Frankfurt School. Fromm finally broke with the Institute in 1940. Other members of the inner circle clearly envied his popularity, though there were legitimate political and philosophical disagreements with him as well. By the end of his life, he had little to do with any of his former associates at the Institute. As much as any member of the Frankfurt School, however, Erich Fromm remained true to the concrete moment, the humanistic spirit, and the transformative purpose of critical theory.

Herbert Marcuse was his only real competitor as an intellectual influence on the New Left. Marcuse's political history reaches back over his time with the Office of Strategic Services from 1941 until the 1950s, where he played an important and progressive role in shaping American policy toward Western Europe, to his participation as a young man in the Spartacus Revolt of 1918–19. His early essays sought to link historical materialism with "historicity," or the phenomenological structures whereby social reality is experienced by the individual. Similar concerns informed Hegel's *Ontology and the Theory of Historicity* (1932), which contributed to a growing Hegel renaissance in Europe, while *Reason and Revolution* (1941) offered a seminal interpretation of the great thinker's relevance for critical theory. Marcuse also authored a number of stunning essays collections. Always cognizant of the utopian potential exhibited by art, yet still concerned with practical forms of resistance, Marcuse envisioned a break with the established order. Nevertheless, his speculative ventures were complemented by various sociological and political studies.

After joining the Institute for Social Research in 1933, Marcuse interrogated the liberal state, the connection between monopoly capitalism and fascism, and the degeneration of communism. His later work anticipated the role of the new social movements in response to the alienation of advanced industrial society. Optimistic concerning the prospects for change in 1968, he also envisioned the conservative reaction that followed. Concepts like the happy consciousness, repressive de-sublimation, and the great refusal were all popularized by him. His signature work, *One-Dimensional Man* (1964), virtually brought critical theory to the United States and, through its citations, introduced many young intellectuals to the Frankfurt School. Marcuse always saw himself as working within the tradition of historical materialism.

But he was flexible in his approach and was a prophet of cultural transformation. Herbert Marcuse incarnated the radical political moment of critical theory for a generation of young radicals in the United States and much of the world.

Walter Benjamin was—by contrast—unknown in the United States until the preeminent political theorist Hannah Arendt published a portrait of him in the *New Yorker* and edited his sterling collection of essays, *Illuminations* (1969). Benjamin thereafter became celebrated as a unique thinker of brilliance and uncanny insight. Another anthology of his essays, *Reflections* (1986), strengthened that assessment. Benjamin's writings range from his lovely autobiographical works *One-Way Street* (1928) and *Berlin Childhood Around 1900* (1950), which appeared originally as a set of newspaper articles in the 1930s, to an abstruse study of the Baroque titled *The Origins of German Tragic Drama* (1928) and his unfinished *Arcades Project* (1982), which comprised a few thousand quotations and offered a veritable hall of mirrors for understanding modernity. With the new popularity accorded postmodernism and other forms of philosophical subjectivism in the United States during the late 1970s, Benjamin's fame soon reached epic proportions: a library of secondary works has appeared, and almost every volume of his *Selected Writings* has become an academic bestseller.

Benjamin was another son from a wealthy Jewish family. Born in Berlin, he received his doctorate from the University of Bern in 1919. He then became an itinerant writer and never held a steady job. There is a sense in which Benjamin incarnated the Luftmensch—the impractical individual whose imagination has lifted him beyond the world. His work was marked by a preoccupation with the fungible character of language, the nature of memory, and the seemingly mundane experiences of everyday life like eating, storytelling, and book collecting. All of these, Benjamin believed, shed light on broader social trends. His explicitly political writings were uninspired and, as exemplified by the Moscow Diary of 1926–27, they offer little insight into the monumental events of his time. But it is a different matter when it comes to his studies on the poetry of Charles Baudelaire, the *Elective Affinities* by J. W. von Goethe, or the novels of Franz Kafka and Marcel Proust. The same holds for Benjamin's articles on architecture, photography, romanticism, and translation. His fascinating and provocative essays explore the aesthetic impact of modernity on individual experience and everyday life.

Influenced by both Gershom Scholem, his childhood friend who became a legendary scholar of Jewish mysticism, and the Marxist playwright Bertolt Brecht, Benjamin attempted to fuse a messianic outlook with what became a growing interest in historical materialism. Reacting against the fatalism of scientific socialism, contemptuous of its transformation of the classless society into an unattainable ideal, his concern was with reclaiming the metaphysical experience of reality and, ultimately, the unrealized utopian possibilities of history. That undertaking was plagued by an inability to articulate the barriers to liberation as well as the inconsistencies and mutually exclusive assumptions embedded in his general outlook. Yet there is little doubt that Walter Benjamin continues to inspire, frustrate, and educate especially young bohemian and radical intellectuals. His writings evoke exile in an age of "ruins," and his tragic suicide in 1940, while attempting to flee the Nazi invasion of France, puts a particularly dramatic stamp on his life.

Walter Benjamin had only one student, Theodor W. Adorno, who embodied the interdisciplinary ideal of the Frankfurt School and the image of the European intellectual. He seemed to know everything—and better than anyone else. Also born into a bourgeois family, but with a Jewish father and an Italian mother, Adorno received his doctorate in 1924. A musicologist who had studied with the great composer Alban Berg, and who was deeply influenced by Arnold Schönberg, Adorno edited a music journal during the 1920s and 1930s, and he later advised Thomas Mann on the sections dealing with music theory in *Doctor Faustus* (1947). Interpretations of great composers like Ludwig von Beethoven, Richard Wagner, and Gustav Mahler followed along with the classic *Philosophy of Modern Music* (1949).

Adorno was also a sensitive critic of literature and poetry and, arguably, was the most dazzling philosophical mind of the age. Committed to the notion of a negative dialectic, deeply skeptical of all systems and traditional understandings of narrative, he was intent upon articulating the inherently flawed character of civilization while rejecting every attempt to identify the individual with the collectivity.

Adorno wove these themes into his own all-embracing philosophical narrative. But he was also engaged in empirical research. Adorno's studies of radio and television, which illuminated the ideological impact of what most considered simple entertainment, complemented his work on the authoritarian and conformist tendencies of modern society. And he was a genuine master of the essay. His "On Popular Music" (1932) demonstrated the impact of the commodity form on the genre while his insightful and innovative interpretations of Beckett, Kafka, and Proust evinced his broader concern with a reflective understanding of experience.

Adorno sometimes dealt with political issues. But he was always fearful of mass movements. Negation assumed a value in its own right, and he identified resistance with securing the "non-identity" between the individual and society. Adorno's influence on contemporary understandings of critical theory is without parallel. No thinker better exemplifies its uncompromising commitment to the glimmer of freedom.

A word still needs to be said about Jürgen Habermas. This most exceptional student of Horkheimer and Adorno became the most prolific of all thinkers associated with the Frankfurt School. His writings touch upon all facets of social life, including religion, and his essays extend from interpretations of the philosophical canon to commentaries on the issues of the day. If his early works made important contributions to critical theory, however, his intellectual path ultimately led him in new directions.

Growing up under Nazism, which other members of the Frankfurt School did not, left Habermas with a deep belief in the rule of law and liberal democracy. It also marked his concern with the manipulation of discourse and the importance of "undistorted communication." These themes run through all his works. An important figure in the student movement of the 1960s, though never engaged with any of its extremist factions, his early writings offer critical meditations on historical materialism, institutional legitimacy, and the relation between theory and practice. The later writings of Habermas, by contrast, are increasingly enmeshed in analytic philosophy. They insist upon the need for grounding claims, formulating systemic arguments, and providing ontological characterizations of nature and science. The extent to which they break with critical theory is a matter of ongoing debate. Making that judgment, indeed, calls for examining the impulses animating the original enterprise.

Coda

The Frankfurt School was marked by a multiplicity in unity. Each member of its inner circle was different. Each had his particular interests and unique intellectual strengths and weaknesses. But they all shared a commitment to the same cluster of themes and concerns. No member of the inner circle ever identified freedom with any system, collectivity, or tradition—and all of them were skeptical about establishmentarian modes of thinking. All of them sought to deal with new problems by introducing new categories. Critical theory in their hands was marked by intellectual daring and an experimental quality. It was for them, in the first instance, always a matter of method. Horkheimer put it well when he wrote: "Critical theory in its concept formation and in all phases of its development very consciously makes its own that concern for the rational organization of human activity which its task is to illuminate and legitimate. For this theory is not concerned only with goals already imposed by existing ways of life, but with men and all their potentialities."

Chapter 2
A matter of method

Critical theory was coined as a term only in 1937. The Frankfurt School was by then in exile in the United States. Fearing political ostracism in their new home, while seeking to secure the Institute, its members employed the term as a cover. Critical theory had, after all, arisen within the framework provided by Western Marxism. Communists like Georg Lukács and Karl Korsch—who had been involved with the Institute from its inception—were among its leading representatives. Ernst Bloch also fits prominently into this tradition. All of them were inspired by the Bolshevik seizure of power in 1917 and the euphoria surrounding the European radical uprisings of 1918–1923.

Advocates of direct action by the working class, skeptical of parliamentary reformism, these activist intellectuals stressed the role of ideology in maintaining capitalism and the decisive character of class consciousness in overturning it. They highlighted the legacy of philosophical idealism for historical materialism as well as the link between Hegel and Marx. Western Marxists had no use for talk about textual orthodoxy or the fixed character of historical materialism. Lukács put the matter succinctly—and laid the basis for all future understandings of critical theory—in his great work, *History and Class Consciousness* (1923), when he wrote:

Let us assume for the sake of argument that recent research had disproved once and for all every one of Marx's individual theses. Even if this were to be proved, every serious "orthodox" Marxist would still be able to accept all such modern findings without reservation.... Orthodox Marxism does not imply the uncritical acceptance of the results of Marx's investigations. It is not the "belief" in this or that thesis, nor the exegesis of a "sacred" book. On the contrary, orthodoxy refers exclusively to method.

Lukács had been a preeminent figure of cultural modernism in Hungary prior to World War I. He soon became perhaps the most prominent intellectual of the communist movement. *History and Class Consciousness* was the seminal work of Western Marxism, and it inspired virtually every major thinker in the critical tradition. But it is easy to understand why Lukács , Korsch, and other Western Marxists were condemned at the Fifth Congress of the Communist International in 1924. Their writings reflected the heroic years of the revolution: its workers councils, cultural experiments, and messianic hopes. They also undercut the certainty associated with scientific versions of socialism by sharply separating the inquiry into society from any inquiry into nature. In fact, Lukács liked to quote Giambatista Vico (1668–1744) that "the difference between history and nature is that man has created the one but not the other." With its utopian vision, its critical attitude toward finished philosophical systems, and its insistence upon proletarian empowerment, Western Marxism was expressive of what Bloch termed "the underground history of the revolution."

Human emancipation became its aim. The critical method was intent upon contesting "hegemony"—using the term made famous by Antonio Gramsci in his *Prison Notebooks* (published posthumously in 1971)—in all its forms. Among the founding members of the Italian Communist Party, who would languish and then die in prison at the hands of Benito Mussolini, Gramsci was not a major influence on the Frankfurt School, but his work throws Western Marxism into sharp relief.

Fundamentally concerned with civil society, its non-economic institutions, and its guiding ideas, he stressed how the dominant culture produces habits of subservience on the part of the ruled. He maintained that a counter-hegemonic strategy was required to empower the working class and, through new civic institutions, strengthen its self-administrative capacities. Such a strategy called for organization not merely from above, or through some rigid vanguard party divorced from the masses, but rather through the practical work of organic intellectuals dialectically bound to the proletariat.

Western Marxists shared this basic outlook. All of them were activists. All of them interpreted historical materialism as a theory of practice that should prove less descriptive than proscriptive. Their point was to clarify the changing conditions and preconditions for transformative action. That standpoint made it illegitimate for Marxists to carry over ideas and categories from one period to the next in mechanical fashion. Or, to put the matter another way, they forced historical materialism to exhibit its historical character.

Karl Korsch made a significant contribution to this view in *Marxism and Philosophy*. Clearly the least known representative of Western Marxism, he interpreted ideology less as some reflex of the economy than as lived experience that would impact upon action. Empowerment of the exploited rested upon consciousness, education, and practical experience. Radicalized by the Russian Revolution, inspired by the spontaneous upsurge of soviets and workers' councils, Korsch fostered a blueprint for radical economic democracy in his pamphlet *What Is Socialization?* (1919). He joined the German Communist Party (KPD) in 1920, assumed the post of minister of justice in Thuringia during the proletarian uprisings of 1923, and became an important influence upon organizationally homeless ultra-left intellectuals after he was purged from the Communist International in 1926.

The Materialist Conception of History (1929) was an attack upon all scientific understandings of Marxism, and Korsch never surrendered his belief in the need for proletarian empowerment. His last book, *Karl Marx* (1938), was a superb intellectual biography. Insisting that any idea can be interpreted for reactionary purposes, wishing to subject the communist revolutionary practices to its own ideals, Korsch highlighted the methodological importance of "historical specification." He treated Marxism no differently than any other form of philosophy. Its character and employment at any given time were understood in terms of the organizational interests, constraints, and opportunities for action provided by the historical context. No longer could it serve as an official dogma or as an immutable system with transcendental claims. Marxism, too, was open to manipulation—and critique.

In the 1937 essay "Traditional and Critical Theory," Horkheimer built upon these views. He considered the new outlook neither a finished logical system nor a set of fixed claims. Concerned with illuminating the neglected aspects of freedom, insistent upon the historically constituted character of reality, and already skeptical about the liberating mission of the proletariat, he conceived of critical theory as an alternative to the dominant philosophical paradigms. Other forms of thought were seen as affirmative of the existing order in spite of their self-proclaimed neutrality and objectivity. Insofar as they ignored its historically constituted character and the possibility of an alternative (whether consciously or unconsciously), they were seen as justifying its workings.

Traditional theory was, therefore neither as neutral nor as reflective as its advocates tended to believe. Social interests were hidden within the philosophical discourse and, if only for this reason, the established approaches could not simply be dismissed out of hand. Immanent criticism was required to demonstrate how the premises of contending philosophical outlooks were tainted by the values of the existing order.

Horkheimer had already confronted two popular strains of mainstream philosophy in these terms with his seminal essay "Materialism and Metaphysics" (1933). Materialism in the form of positivism and its offshoots was condemned for dismissing subjectivity and ethical concerns while analyzing society through categories and criteria derived from the natural sciences. Metaphysics was, by contrast, castigated for ignoring the philosophical relevance of the material world and employing universal precepts to enable the individual—whether through what Kant termed "practical reason" or what Heidegger understood as phenomenology—to indulge in what are ultimately intuitive moral judgments.

These seemingly opposed philosophical outlooks were seen by Horkheimer as flip sides of the same coin. Each is mechanically defined by what it opposes. Yet they converge in their contemplative preoccupation with philosophical foundations, unalterable categories for interpreting reality, and fixed notions for verifying experience or truth claims. To be sure, scientific rationality was considered the more pernicious of the two by the Frankfurt School. Nevertheless, its members originally chastised them both for their blindness to critical reflection, history, and the utopian imagination.

Critical theory was intended as a general theory of society fueled by the desire for liberation. Its practitioners understood that new social conditions would give rise to new ideas and new problems for radical practice—and that the character of the critical method would change along with the substance of emancipation. Highlighting the context for practice thus became a core concern for the new interdisciplinary approach of the Frankfurt School. In turn, this led its members to reject the traditional separation between facts and values.

Critical theory would treat facts less as isolated depictions of reality than as crystallized historical products of social action. The aim was to understand a fact within the value-laden context wherein it assumes meaning. Lukács had already placed the category of totality, or what Marx termed "the ensemble of social relations," at the center of historical materialism. The totality was seen as comprised of various moments with the economy serving as merely one among others like the state and a cultural realm that itself could be divided into religion, art, and philosophy. Each moment is shaped by the totality but each is also understood as having its unique dynamic and, as a consequence, an impact upon the practice of those agents (like the working class) intent upon transforming reality. Each moment thus needs to be taken seriously.

Fromm made this idea his starting point in "Psychoanalysis and Sociology" (1929) and "Politics and Psychoanalysis" (1930). These two early essays noted the impact of society on how the ego is organized, how the psychic apparatus affects the development of society, and the extent to which psychology can aid the political confrontation with inhuman conditions. Fromm also sought to show how psychological attitudes mediated the relation between the individual and society.

Escape from Freedom, his most famous work, analyzed the market character generated by capitalist society and its sadomasochistic variant as a specific response to the cultural crisis of the Weimar Republic. This work spoke to the alienating impulses of modern life that produced the desire to identify totally with a leader. His materialist psychology already found expression during the late 1920s in *The Working Class in Weimar Germany*, a massive empirical study that dealt with the debilitating impact of traditional attitudes, familial relations, and social life on revolutionary class consciousness.

Critical theory resurrected the concern with ideology and its practical impact. *History and Class Consciousness* showed how an unacknowledged class standpoint prevented even the giants of bourgeois thought from dealing with the social causes of alienation and reification. Korsch insisted, meanwhile, that all the variants of Marxism needed to be seen in relation to developments in the labor movement at any particular point in time. The Frankfurt School began to analyze mass culture, the state, reactionary sexual mores, and even philosophy with regard to their effects on consciousness. Highlighting how everyday artifacts illuminate the character of society and the cultural trends of an epoch quickly proved of particular interest for its members and associates. Critical theory sought to make good on the injunction of the young Marx and engage in a "ruthless critique of everything existing." Its leading representatives insisted that the whole could be seen in the particular and the particular reflected the whole.

"The Mass Ornament" (1927) by Siegfried Kracauer, for example, noted how the geometric patterns and highly orchestrated

3. The Tiller Girls danced in tightly orchestrated geometric patterns that seemed to reflect the increasing administration and standardization of modern society.

movements of a dance troupe known as the Tiller Girls (anticipating the Rockettes of Radio City Music Hall) reflected the regulation of audiences and the loss of individuality in mass society.

Close friends with Benjamin and Adorno, and loosely associated with the Frankfurt School, Kracauer authored a self-styled "social biography"—*Jacques Offenbach and the Paris of His Time* (1937)—that placed the music of the great composer in the context of the parliamentary revolt of 1832 with an eye on the antifascist Popular Front. His classic *From Caligari to Hitler* (1947), meanwhile, would illustrate how Nazi themes increasingly penetrated the German films of the Weimar Republic.

Other thinkers followed suit. "The Storyteller" (1936) by Walter Benjamin discussed the erosion of the oral tradition and the imperiled character of historical experience in relation to the new technological possibilities for reproducing art in modern society. "Lyric Poetry and Society" (1957) by Theodor W. Adorno innovatively interpreted the ideological residues of a poetic genre usually considered insulated from external forces. In a similar vein, Leo Lowenthal viewed the increasing lack of individuality among movie stars as reflecting the growing power of the commodity form in his essay collection, *Literature and Mass Culture* (published 1984). He also offered an elegant sociological inquiry into the emergence of the bourgeois mentality through major literary characters in *Literature and the Image of Man* (published 1986).

All of these works evince the influence of the sociology of knowledge whose leading figure, Karl Mannheim, held seminars in the Institute for Social Research. His major work, *Ideology and Utopia* (1931), argued that even the most universal and utopian mode of thought is ideological insofar as it inherently reflects the interests of a particular social group or class. Only the "free-floating intelligentsia" is seen by Mannheim (who was also deeply influenced by Lukacs) as capable of grasping the totality.

Horkheimer dealt with all of this in "The Social Function of Philosophy" (1939). He objected to the mechanical reduction of philosophy to sociology. Significantly, however, he avoided directly confronting the idea of a free-floating intelligentsia. That only makes sense. Horkheimer took pride in the political independence of the Institute. He also maintained that the critique of ideology employs speculative norms for judging how ideas express particular social interests. It evaluates cultural phenomena in terms of both how they justify the existing order and contest the abolition of exploitation and unhappiness.

Critical theory can be understood as presenting a version of the sociology of knowledge with a transformative intent Marx had understood capitalism as an economic system in which the working class serves as the producer of wealth (or capital). If only for this reason, the proletariat constitutes the only force capable of transforming the system. In *The Communist Manifesto* (1848), however, Marx and Engels insisted that revolutions are possible only if elements of the ruling class break off and join the struggle of the oppressed. Insofar as the working class is entrapped by capitalism, and material misery stunts its consciousness, bourgeois intellectuals are needed to provide the proletariat with a systemic critique of capitalism and consciousness of its revolutionary possibilities. Lenin drew the radical implications.

The Frankfurt School was sympathetic to communism during the 1930s. Its members did not yet offer an outright critique of technological rationality. They were content to argue that the dominance of instrumental reason was merely an expression of capitalist social relations. As communism turned totalitarian, however, the Frankfurt School became disillusioned, and its critique of the reification process intensified. The Hitler-Stalin Pact of 1939 that unleashed World War II was the last straw. Practice had betrayed theory. The teleological claims of historical materialism now seemed as barren as the ethical imperatives of idealism. Social transformation was no longer the issue.

Totalitarianism turned the preservation of individuality into the central preoccupation of critical theory.

New motivations and forms of resistance were required. Horkheimer's early collection of aphorisms, *Dawn*, had already interpreted empathy and compassion as concrete needs and as ethical impulses for action. His thinking was in accord with the criticism that David Hume once made with regard to the philosophy of Kant: animals should be protected, the great Scottish philosopher claimed, not because they think but because they suffer. Emotional experience was thus interpreted as a source of resistance and liberation. Benjamin wrote about how surrealism with its reliance on the powers of the unconscious generates a revolutionary "intoxication" that responds to a stultifying "poverty of the interior."

Adorno gave his *Minima Moralia* (1951) the subtitle "reflections of a damaged life." Issues of love and personal fulfillment would play an ever more profound role in Fromm's later writings while Marcuse ultimately developed the idea of a "new sensibility" in *An Essay on Liberation* (1972). The Frankfurt School was now engaged in redeeming the repressed potential within the lived life of the individual.

Contempt for cruelty and the desire to live an upright existence inspired its intellectual efforts. All its members showed an explicit interest in abolishing not merely social injustice but the psychological, cultural, and anthropological sources of unhappiness. Intellectual support for this undertaking derives from a plethora of sources. The Frankfurt School was audacious in its attempts to assimilate the insights of diverse thinkers into the framework of historical materialism. Its members looked to Freud either for his metapschology, which might underpin their critique of civilization, or for insights deriving from his clinical work. Like the rest of their generation, moreover, leading figures of the Frankfurt School were also inspired by Nietzsche for his resurrection of subjectivity, his "perspectival" approach, his contributions to modernism, and his searing criticisms of the cultural philistine. These thinkers would help deepen the philosophical and cultural outlook of the Frankfurt School. Whether their views fit logically into some prefabricated system of historical materialism was considered immaterial.

Walter Benjamin actually sought to refashion Marxism by framing its revolutionary commitments in theological terms. In his "Theses on the Philosophy of History," written shortly before his death in 1940, the Messiah can appear at any moment in time; exigencies and constraints give way before the possibilities of the pregnant "now-time" (*Jetztzeit*); the revolution becomes an apocalyptic "leap into the open skies of history." Indications of how all this might be achieved—or even what is concretely implied—are lacking. Symbols trump reality: the imagination runs wild. Redeeming the forgotten moments of history now becomes the goal of critique. Benjamin conceived of history as "one single catastrophe that keeps piling wreckage upon wreckage." Only from the standpoint of a messianic materialism are the shards of that catastrophe open to redemption.

Gershom Scholem was on target when he called his friend a "theologian marooned in the realm of the profane." What remains from Benjamin's investigations is less an explicit method than an ill-fated attempt to blend the theological reclamation of experience with the revolutionary kernel of historical materialism. He often made use of modernist techniques, and he was inspired by the emphasis upon subjectivity offered not only by expressionism and surrealism but by romanticism and the baroque. His injunction to "never forget the best" was coupled with his desire to "rub history against the grain." Discarded fragments reveal the possibility for an apocalyptic redemption of undefined stature that might occur at any moment—or, more likely, never.

Everyday life serves as the material for utopia, and no preconceived plan or set of universal concepts can suffice for its determination. Utopia derives from the imaginative will to reconfigure what Benjamin called the "rubbish" of history—the look of a forgotten boulevard, postage stamps, children's literature, eating, collecting books, the euphoria of hashish, memories of revolutionaries shooting at the clocks. Montage and stream of consciousness were most appropriate for generating the kind of "revolutionary intoxication" that led those radical street-fighters of 1789 to indeed shoot at clocks embedded in the towers above them. The real changes its face in the light of future redemption. The imaginative will—theological in origin—shatters the material constraints of history. Each moment of time is the door through which the Messiah might pass.

The question is how best to open it. To remember the best requires a distinctly hermeneutical approach predicated on the assumption that "allegory is to language what ruins are to things." Civilization offers only hints and traces of what utopia must redeem. In keeping with the famous painting *Angelus Novus* (1920) by Paul Klee, wherein the angel of history with face turned to the past is nonetheless propelled into the future. Benjamin owned the painting and was proud of it. That painting ultimately became an icon of the Left. In his "Theses on the Philosophy of History," Benjamin described this angel in the following way:

> His face is turned toward the past. Where we perceive a chain of events, he sees one single catastrophe which keeps piling ruin upon ruin and hurls it in front of his feet. The angel would like to stay, awaken the dead, and make whole what has been smashed. But a storm is blowing from paradise; it has got caught in his wings with such violence that the angel can no longer close them. The storm irresistibly propels him into the future to which his back is turned, while the pile of debris before him grows skyward. This storm is what we call progress.

Redemption is now the key to utopia. Critique recalls what history forgets by rummaging around the ruins and putting the garbage to use in sparking the imagination. The totality now makes way for a "constellation" of juxtaposed empirical facts that illuminates a particular theme or concept for which members of the audience must provide ever-changing connections and interpretations. Benjamin's unfinished and posthumously published *Arcades Project* is an expression of this outlook. Its attempt to offer an "ur-history of modernity," by providing thousands of quotations without authorial commentary, projects a transcendent narrative constructed through fragments and fashioned with an ever-shifting gaze on the reader's desire. Existing within an experiential "horizon," seemingly preserved from the imposition of external categories, these quotations constitute a grand montage. If the totally administered society is standardizing thought by rendering it formulaic, then redemption cannot be found in the simple narrative form. Only aphorisms or fragments allow for the evanescent moment in which utopian glimpses can be illuminated. The mediated totality surrenders in favor of the individually structured constellation as the organizing principle of critical theory.

"The Actuality of Philosophy," which Adorno presented as his inaugural lecture to the Institute in 1931, used it to challenge the totalizing outlook of Hegel and Marx. The constellation offers no structured narrative or overarching logic that might provide a consensual view of what is being presented. Each member of the audience can put an interpretive stamp on the fragments as if he or she were looking at a collage or surrealist painting. Benjamin's *Arcades Project* crystallizes the constellation. His interpretation of modernity contests the rational presumptions of a seemingly integrated world that is actually dominated by rupture and incoherence.

Critical theory shifts its focus: its aim is now to awaken the individual from the intellectual slumber into which he or she has been socialized. Subjectivity is no longer considered identical with or capable of being defined by any category. In *The Jargon of Authenticity* (1964), for example, Adorno insists that even existential phenomenology standardizes experience and that ontologically structured intuitions—especially of the sort connected with dying and death—substitute individuation for individuality. Divorcing experience from critical reflection creates an opening for ideology and compromises the ability to resist what Adorno termed the "ontology of false conditions." But the assault on system, logic, and narrative by Benjamin and Adorno carry a price: it undermines the ability to generate criteria for making ethical and political judgments thereby threatening to plunge critical theory into relativism.

In *The Philosophical Discourse of Modernity* (1987), Jürgen Habermas sought to confront these philosophical problems. He questioned the emphasis on a free-floating subjectivity of resistance and insisted upon explicit foundations for any genuinely critical theory of society. Better to rely on the structure of language—or communicative action—for grounding reciprocity, reflection, and universality. But this form of critique gives too much ground to establishmentarian forms of philosophy. It remains stuck in analytic concerns–the argument remains defined by what it should oppose.

Max Weber was one of the most important influences on critical theory in general and the Frankfurt School in particular. He never wrote a work fully articulating his method and the debate continues with regard to its character. His healthy skepticism of treating practical matters in metaphysical terms, however, serves as a useful corrective for the aesthetic and philosophical obsessions that have shaped critical theory in our supposedly postmetaphysical age. Toward the end of his life, indeed, Weber supposedly remarked that: "Method is the most sterile of all concerns....Nothing was ever accomplished through method alone." He was right.

The Frankfurt School originally saw itself articulating a new form of materialism infused with critical reflection, a capacity for fantasy, and the prospect of resisting an increasingly bureaucratized world. But it became ever less clear what practical purposes its speculative inquiries were meant to serve. The understanding of resistance grew increasingly vague. It was as if the real conflicts of interest, the real imbalances of power, were vanishing within a totality defined by alienation and reification.

Chapter 3
Alienation and reification

An extraordinary intellectual event took place in 1932. That was the year in which Karl Marx's *Economic and Philosophic Manuscripts of 1844* were finally published, accompanied by a superb review from Herbert Marcuse, in the Institute's *Journal for Social Research*. The collection had been smuggled out of the Marx-Engels Institute in Moscow by its director, David Ryazanov, who was obviously risking his life, considering the political climate at that time. These manuscripts, when coupled with other writings of the young Marx, quickly achieved international renown. They served to justify many of the arguments made by Western Marxism in general and Georg Lukács in particular.

The writings by the young Marx evidence a utopian quality. They give precedence to the anthropological and existential elements of human misery rather than capitalist exploitation of a purely economic sort. Alienation has its roots in an inability to grasp the workings of history and subject them to human control. The division of labor expresses this situation. It leaves workers increasingly divorced from the products they produce, their fellows with whom they work, and—ultimately—their possibilities as individuals. Eliminating private property is thus not an end unto itself but only a stepping stone to claiming control over history.

The young Marx offers an apocalyptic vision. Political emancipation in the liberal state is subordinated to the ideal of human emancipation in a classless, free association of producers. Fostering individual autonomy—perhaps *the* ethical aim of the revolutionary bourgeoisie—is assimilated into a concern with realizing the new communal and organic notion of "species being." Improving working conditions in a world of scarcity, or "necessity," makes way for a "leap into the realm of freedom." Alienation and, implicitly, reification now become the targets of radical activity. Ideas such as these transformed the popular understanding of Marxism, gravely embarrassed the communist regime, and inspired the Frankfurt School no less than the intellectual radicals of 1968.

The roots of unhappiness

Alienation has a long history. Its connection with utopia already appears in the biblical expulsion of from Eden. The story of paradise lost precedes the loss of objects to the world of commodity exchange. The biblical allegory justifies the fallen state of humanity and explains why people are condemned "to earn their bread by the sweat of their brow." It also shows why trust between individuals has been lost, nature appears as an enemy, and—interestingly enough—redemption becomes possible. Unity and harmony are forfeited. Adam and Eve exhibited free will. They brought about their expulsion from Eden—by succumbing to evil. Perhaps different choices might bring about the re-creation of paradise. Prometheus may have sought to make good on that hope: there is a reason why he was Marx's favorite mythical character. But Prometheus was condemned for his hubris by a wicked god as surely as those who sought to build the Tower of Babel.

Paradise has always been identified with the pastoral. The garden was the world in which the organic connection between humanity and nature was secured. The arts and sciences, wealth, and technology may foster civilization but—as Jean-Jacques Rousseau famously argued in his *Discourse on the Arts and Sciences* (1750)—they fragment the organic community and produce an antagonistic relationship between humanity and nature. Artificial needs are thereby created that corrupt the natural virtues like decency, simplicity, kindness, and honesty. Only a thoroughly regenerated society might restore these values and overcome the loneliness and sense of meaninglessness experienced by individuals—as well as the prospect of death.

A host of thinkers from St. Augustine to Rousseau, and especially Rousseau's followers among the Romantics, explored these themes. The basic idea is perhaps best expressed by Friedrich Hölderlin—a close of friend of the young Hegel and much beloved by later critical theorists—who wrote in *Hyperion* (1795):

> You see craft-workers, but no genuine people; thinkers but
> no people; priests, but no people; lords and servants,
> youths and persons of property but no people. Is this
> world not like a battlefield on which hands, arms, and
> limbs of all sorts lie strewn amid one another while
> their spilled life-blood runs into the sands?

Yet, it was G. W. F. Hegel who offered the first systematic analysis of alienation. He believed that alienation exists insofar as humanity is estranged from its normative ends, and its creations escape its conscious control. World history is the stigmata suffered by consciousness whose purpose is to appropriate anew what humanity has unwittingly produced. Rooting alienation within the structure of consciousness can be seen as insulating it from reality. But Hegel's recognition of the subjective powers lurking behind the world of objects expressed the fundamental desire of idealism that the estranged world should be transformed into a human one. Hegel's principal concern was the way in which social action escapes conscious direction and history occurs, so to speak, behind the back of humanity.

Entire civilizations appear and disappear, consequences are turned against intentions, and the finest achievements of intellectual life and politics are paid for in blood. Hegel understood history as a "slaughter-bench" even though the realization of human freedom is pre-ordained. Such a realm can be defined as one in which each individual is fully recognized as a subject in his or her own right. Universal reciprocity ultimately becomes incarnated in a bureaucratic state under the rule of law, a civil society based on the market in which all enter freely and equally, and a nuclear family in which each subject is emotionally embraced as such. Reason projects such a realm of all-inclusive reciprocity because philosophy, the highest incarnation of reason, was believed by Hegel to embody a sense of universality from the time of Socrates.

Abolishing alienation thus involves redeeming the miseries of history, which Hegel called the "Calvary of the absolute spirit." But he was no utopian. Realizing freedom is the culmination of a teleological process wherein the arbitrary exercise of power is negated in a new state governed by the rule of law. Conflict and existential alienation remain even at the "end of history" insofar as individuals must still confront their own mortality. The constitutional state simply creates the space in which they can finally concentrate upon their most private concerns free of external interference. Alienation and reification continue to exist in the exploitative class relations of civil society.

Hegel's thinking remains stuck at the level of the state. This is due not merely to class interest. His inability to deal with alienation in terms of its roots in the capitalist production process also has an existential component: to engage the material character of alienation would involve denying the bourgeois aims of his entire project. Alienation thus finds its way into the philosophy seeking to abolish it. Workers councils, the classless society, and the end of what Marx termed "pre-history" are not on the agenda. Even the greatest bourgeois philosophers were incapable of envisioning political institutions capable of subordinating the workings of society to those who produce it.

Hegel noted in *The Phenomenology of Mind* (1807) that the lords and masters of every historical epoch have an existential and material interest in preventing such consciousness from coming about. They seek to make their servants and slaves believe in their dependence upon them, their masters, through ideological and institutional means. This was the point of departure for Hegel and the young Marx. The critical method becomes the tool by which the servants and the slaves—and the masses of the proletariat—realize their power as producers of the particular order from which the lords and masters alone genuinely benefit. Abolishing alienation thus depends upon the consciousness of the slave—or, better, the worker.

The young Marx believed that talk about the virtues of the state, or realizing some prefabricated idea of freedom through imprecise categories like master and slave, or rich and poor, only stunts consciousness about the source of alienation and how it is maintained. In the *Economic and Philosophic Manuscripts of 1844*, therefore, Marx insisted that "only when the objective world becomes everywhere for man in society the world of man's essential powers—human reality, and for that reason, the reality of his own essential powers—can all objects become for him the objectification of himself, become objects which confirm and realize his individuality."

Hegel claimed that the whole is true. He argued that freedom had been realized in the bourgeois state under the liberal rule of law. According to Marx, however, the proletariat contests this assumption. The very existence of this disenfranchised and exploited class demonstrates how freedom has been truncated. The structural domination of this class is ignored. Capitalism is understood by the bourgeois as resting on egoistic assumptions with the individual as the primary unit of productive activity. But this view makes it become impossible to conceptualize the constitution of social reality and the contradictions of its economic production process. If religion produces a situation in which humanity is dominated by the products of its brain, which is what Marx learned from Ludwig Feuerbach, then, under capitalism, humanity is dominated by the products of its hands.

Marx believed that the working class was growing poorer even while bourgeois society was growing richer. The proletariat was also becoming more spiritually impoverished. It was becoming an appendage of the machine. Individuality, creativity, solidarity were all being eroded for the great bulk of humanity. The imperatives of capitalist production call for viewing it merely as a cost of production that must be kept as minimal as possible. Maximizing profits also requires the division of labor whereby each member of the working class is separated from others on the assembly line, kept from learning other tasks and developing his or her full potential, and conceptualizing the product that is ultimately being produced. This same division of labor infects the modern state. Mathematical formulae define profitability and efficiency in transhistorical terms without recognizing structural conflicts of class interest. Society is thereby robbed of its historical, fungible, and changeable character.

Alienation defines the totality whose perpetuation rests on turning people into things—or reification. Capitalism increasingly strips human beings of their humanity. It treats the real subject engaged in the production of commodities (the proletariat) as an object even as it turns the real object of its productive activity (capital) into the fictive subject of modern life. Inverting this "inverted world"—an idea that Marx borrowed from Hegel—is possible only by abolishing what in *Das Kapital* is termed "commodity fetishism." Or putting it somewhat differently, abolishing alienation calls for abolishing reification. This requires

4. Alienation and reification destroy subjectivity and turn the worker into a cost of production.

consciousness of what is to be transformed. The world must be thought anew.

The young Marx raised the revolutionary stakes. Human misery is the target of radical action even if capitalism increasingly brings it to fruition. Bureaucracy, money, and instrumental thinking have anthropological roots even if the new production process intensifies their dominance. The lowly and the insulted have been treated instrumentally since time immemorial. The commodity form and bureaucracy reach back to the stock exchange of ancient Rome and the hierarchy of the Roman Catholic Church. The implication is clear. Workers cannot remain content with the desire for liberal democracy, social reform, and narrow calculation of economic interest, The proletariat must now understand itself as the subject of historical action—not merely the object of external forces—whose purpose is the abolition of alienation and class society.

The young Marx had sketched this vision. Insofar as his writings were unknown prior to 1932, however, the seminal influence on Lukács and later on other critical theorists in formulating (if not solving!) the problems of alienation and reification was Max Weber. A tortured academic who authored the classic *Protestant Ethic and the Spirit of Capitalism* (1905), a liberal with nationalist and imperialist sympathies, Weber's famous lecture "Science as a Vocation" (1918) envisioned a world in which the hopes of the Enlightenment were "irretrievably fading" and society was increasingly dominated by "specialists without spirit" and "sensualists without heart." Instrumental rationality employs a mathematically defined notion of efficiency predicated upon rendering all tasks routine. Modern life would increasingly privilege the use of expertise and narrowly circumscribed areas of responsibility within a hierarchical chain of command. The ability to grasp the whole would vanish; what the Germans call the disciplinary idiot would supplant the intellectual; and ethics would be relegated to a domain outside of science and political life. Weber imagined the future as a bureaucratic iron cage—even if he never explicitly used the term so often associated with him—that would ever more surely marginalize authentic subjectivity.

Apocalypse and metaphysics

As young men, Bloch and Lukács frequented Weber's famous salon in Heidelberg where they came to know Emil Lask, Heinrich Rickert, and Georg Simmel. All of them were concerned with the alienated structure of modern society and the implications of reification as well. The influences of Weber and his circle became apparent in the first version of Bloch's *Spirit of Utopia* (1918) and Lukács's *Theory of the Novel* that was written in 1915 and published in 1920. Indeed, Bloch liked to say that he wrote half of the one while Lukács wrote half of the other. Both works exemplify what Lukács later called "romantic anti-capitalism."

The term was meant to identify a critical encounter with capitalism whose ignorance about how it actually functions produces either apocalyptic visions or a withdrawal into the self. That is because romantic anti-capitalism tends to blend left-wing politics with right-wing epistemology. This was surely the case with *Theory of the Novel* and *Spirit of Utopia*. Yet they remain seminal works.

Reflection upon the alienation of modern life, an apocalyptic sensibility, and a withering critique of modernity constitute their intellectual legacy for critical theory. Each stressed the increasing fragmentation of life and that human relations between people were breaking down. Each anticipates a new form of solidarity based on the quest for authentic experience (or better its loss) and an apocalyptic sensibility. Each offers a new philosophy of history that contests positivism and the infatuation with science. Each also champions a kind of aesthetic-philosophical outlook and a new beginning for a Western world that has been plunged into barbarism.

In his little study *Lenin* (1924), Lukács stressed that the Bolshevik leader was marked by his commitment to the "actuality of revolution." *What Is To Be Done?* (1902) by Lenin had championed the idea of a vanguard party of dedicated political intellectuals to preserve the revolutionary ideal from reformist temptations. In 1914, he was alone in calling for the transformation of a war between nations into an international class war. "All Power to the Soviets!" was Lenin's revolutionary slogan in 1917, and his *State and Revolution* (1918) envisioned a communist state that is no longer a state in the proper sense of the word. Lenin's Bolsheviks appeared to usher in a "wind from the East" that was destined to sweep away a decadent civilization. His organizational vision seemed part and parcel of a politics in which everything seemed possible. The proletariat—or, better, the proletariat under the auspices of the vanguard party—might just prove to be the new subject-object of history.

History and Class Consciousness expressed the longing for regeneration and renewal that accompanied the Russian Revolution. It was the same with the writings of Korsch, and also Gramsci, though they lacked the metaphysical apparatus and apocalyptic language. All of them projected the vision of a liberated world arising from the Russian Revolution and the accompanying European uprisings that occurred in its wake from 1918 to 1923. Liberal republicanism paled in comparison with the drama surrounding the participatory democracy of workers' councils, the elimination of money and rank, and the manifold cultural experiments with a utopian flavor. Only a communist vanguard, whatever the empirical consciousness of the actual proletariat, was considered capable kind of bringing the world of alienation to an end.

Following its appearance in 1923, however, *History and Class Consciousness* became the target of intense criticism. Viewing the proletariat (or, better, the communist party) as the subject-object of history was considered a utopian outgrowth of idealism—not Marxism. It was generally believed that Lukács had exaggerated the role of consciousness to the detriment of economics and that his work took little account of concrete goals and the institutional constraints on action. With the publication of Marx's *Economic and Philosophical Manuscripts of 1844*, however, many of Lukács's arguments received belated justification. The Communist International was particularly embarrassed, since its leaders had forced Lukács to renounce his masterpiece in 1924. The writings of the young Marx revivified interest in what most intellectuals tended to consider a rigid and unyielding political ideology.

Alienation became a truly popular concept, however, through *Escape from Freedom* by Erich Fromm. Nazism had become the chief enemy for liberal and progressive intellectuals following the outbreak of World War II in 1939. Fromm showed how the egoistic acquisitive attributes of the "market character" associated with capitalism in the Weimar Republic, was transformed by the new fascist regime into a "sado-masochistic character" predicated on the explicit elimination of autonomy. Its subversion of all public institutions capable of resisting the propaganda of the new regime—that is, mass media, schools, religion, and even the family—left the individual utterly isolated or atomized.

Extreme alienation of this sort is untenable. An identification with authority (i.e., the *Fuhrer*) is thereby generated that leaves the individual filled with hate and yet intent upon avoiding ethical responsibility. A specific confluence of sociological and psychological influences thus gives rise to a uniquely authoritarian personality structure.

Max Horkheimer took a more over-arching approach. His essay "The Authoritarian State" (1940) analyzed the conflation of modern liberalism, communism, and fascism. All of them rely on bureaucratic administration and control, hierarchy and subservience, propaganda and mass culture, the division of labor and mechanized work. The individual is alienated from the product of labor, other workers, and a broader and more encompassing notion of individuality. The totality everywhere escapes from view and reification is the norm insofar as the individual is little more than a cog in the machine. Differences between regime-types might still exist, but, ultimately, the form is the content. With the dashing of teleological hopes once associated with the proletariat, indeed, resistance loses its political referent. The authoritarian state calls the ability to frame a theory of practice into question.

Alienation and reification thus increasingly become understood as psychological and philosophical problems that in the first instance require psychological and philosophical solutions. In *Knowledge and Human Interest* (1971), for example, Jürgen Habermas posited an "ideal speech situation" predicated on "undistorted communication." The ideal becomes concrete in the psychoanalytic encounter where both the analyst and the client, unimpeded by external or material interests, are intent on finding the true source of any given neurosis or pathology. A "generalizable interest" thereby emerges that is lacking in traditional forms of philosophy like positivism and phenomenology.

Critique is now given a positive foundation. Its confrontation with the manipulation of discourse is undertaken from an "emancipatory" basis. This has certain practical implications. Mutual understanding among activists becomes paramount, and each must prove self-critical of his or her goals and tactics. In principle, after all, undistorted communication underpins all forms of deliberative democracy. Older concerns with the historical constitution of reality can now also be treated as technical problems. Habermas made his position clear: "in the power of self-reflection, knowledge and interest are one."

Questions of argumentation and definition, however, quickly arise for this innovative psychological-philosophical approach. Is the ideal speech situation merely a methodological point of departure for social action or is it rather a fixed philosophical category with its own rules? Is it a matter of understanding undistorted communication in terms of a critical theory of society or as the foundation for a new variant of language philosophy with its own rules? Habermas made the "linguistic turn."

Critical theory thus took its first steps into the arena of analytic philosophy. *Theory of Communicative Action* (1981), another classic work by Habermas, admittedly still warns of the dangers posed by instrumental rationality and the institutional forces of late capitalism to the life world of the individual. Communicative action with its linguistic rules, insulated from history, becomes the vehicle for resistance. But the motivation for engaging in it is another matter entirely. Without reference to the production process, or political organization, new concerns with recognition and identity become primary. Demands of this sort, however, often conflict. Axel Honneth the protégé of Habermas, sought to deal with such conflicts emanating from alienation and reification by highlighting the ability of individuals to "care."

Empathy takes center stage insofar as caring involves recognizing the other and constraining the more crass forms of egotism. Alienation and reification are now framed as philosophical and experiential problems in need of a philosophically grounded experiential response. Ethical norms become, once again, severed from the realities of political life. Institutional imbalances of power, structured conflicts of group interest, and the imperatives of capitalist accumulation fade from view. Specifying the constraints on caring and the like, or the appropriate forms of action for dealing with alienation and reification, became matters of secondary interest. The debilitating implications for generating any meaningful notion of solidarity—and resistance—are self-evident.

To be fair, however, most members of the Frankfurt School's inner circle believed that prescribing remedies for alienation and reification (from within the existing system) was useless at best or a compromise of principle at worst. Pessimism became pervasive among the inner circle once the proletariat lost its revolutionary standing. In "Philosophy and Critical Theory" (1937) Marcuse already noted that the dialectic of Hegel and Marx, which rested on the prospect of realizing the realm of freedom, had been stunted and that radical change was no longer on the agenda.

The iron cage of bureaucracy was seemingly bringing about the "end of the individual." This was the vision depicted by Horkheimer in *The Eclipse of Reason* (1940). Capitalism had ceased generating its gravediggers, and totalitarianism was infecting both ends of the political spectrum: Horkheimer stated bluntly that "the extremes meet." Traditional assumptions about socialism and historical progress were therefore in need of revision. A new framework was required to deal with the integrative power of the bureaucratic society, the impotence of organized opposition, the regressive character of progress, and the need—above all else—to cultivate autonomy. If revolution can no longer be identified with liberation, then resistance must change its character. This would ultimately involve confronting civilization, progress, and enlightenment.

Looking backward

Critical theorists saw in the *Economic and Philosophic Manuscripts* a new emphasis upon ending the repression associated with the "pre-history" of humanity. Socialism would now be identified with how people were treated rather than a fixed set of institutions and policies. The young Marx seemed to exhibit utopian inclinations along with the vision of a new man freed from egotism, cruelty, and alienation. The revolution against capitalism now turned into something intent upon transforming the human condition. Critics suggested that it was now impossible to envision what revolutionary success might entail. Understanding revolutionary failure, however, was rendered easier. The newly discovered writings of the young Marx played an important role in challenging a gray and drab understanding of socialism.

Erich Fromm's edition of *Marx's Concept of Man* (1961) became wildly popular, and it inspired a generation of American radicals. Even before that, however, Fromm was preoccupied with the phenomenon of alienation. His various writings on religion and psychology make that clear. Capitalism was to be opposed not simply because it was materially exploitative, but because its system of impersonal market forces called upon individuals to treat one another as potential competitors and means to an end. The issue for him was not merely the mechanized society over which humanity has lost control, but the inner passivity and mental dullness that it fostered. His critical social psychology was thus predicated on articulating and affirming anti-capitalist values and progressive possibilities for individual development. Here is the basis for what would become an overriding attempt to recast socialism as a form of humanism while downplaying narrow class concerns and revolution.

Henry Pachter once told me, however, that his first reaction in 1932 upon reading the *Economic and Philosophic Manuscripts* was: "This is the end of Marxism." He was a socialist activist, a political historian, and also loosely connected with the Frankfurt School. Today a statement like Pachter's sounds strange. But it made sense in the context of the 1930s. Marxism was still understood as an all-embracing philosophical system with scientific foundations and teleological guarantees. An aura hung over the communist movement, and social democracy still seemed to incarnate the only genuine opposition to political dictatorship and social injustice. Both the socialist and the communist movements were less intent upon utopia than nationalizing major industries and regulating the market, substituting a (democratic or authoritarian) dictatorship of the proletariat for the rule of the bourgeoisie, and introducing a new secular ideology presumably based on technological and scientific progress.

The more traditional outlook was far less dramatic than what the new approach offered with its assault on alienation and reification. But there is something enviable in its clarity of purpose and its privileging of politics. There is no need for nostalgia. Its philosophical and political aims were modest only in comparison with the exotic disquisitions and utopian exaggerations that were to follow.

Chapter 4
Enlightened illusions

Max Horkheimer and Theodor Adorno's *Dialectic of Enlightenment* was perhaps the first great critical encounter with modernity undertaken from the Left. It first appeared in a private printing for the Institute with the title *Philosophical Fragments* in 1944. When it was finally published with Querido Verlag in 1947, however, the original title had been turned into the subtitle. The focus had become more precise. Initially that didn't help matters: it sold only about two thousand copies. Today, however, *Dialectic of Enlightenment* is recognized as landmark of modern philosophy and, arguably, the signature work of critical theory. Two very different intellectual temperaments find expression in this book. Its text exhibits complex tensions and various interpretations are possible. Nevertheless, certain features are indisputable.

This work investigates how scientific (or instrumental) rationality expels freedom from the historical process and enables reification to penetrate every aspect of society. Even art turns into just another commodity and loses its critical character. Conformism is now treated by the dialectical discourse as something more than a merely bohemian concern. Metaphysics is, moreover, given an innovative and radical twist. Horkheimer and Adorno respond to the "totally administered society" with a systematic assault on systematic thinking or, better, an anti-narrative that itself becomes a narrative. Their book also provides a sophisticated attempt to employ thinkers outside the enlightenment tradition in order better to understand its limitations. It insists not merely that the price of progress is too high but that barbarism is embedded within civilization and that the Enlightenment has betrayed its most sacred promise: autonomy.

The illusion of progress

Dialectic of Enlightenment was loyal to the imperative of the young Marx that to be genuinely radical is to go to the "root" of a problem. Historically, both in theory and practice, Leftists had basically identified with the Enlightenment project. Even the young Marx, who harbored more than a touch of romanticism, insisted that the proletariat must take its goals from the revolutionary bourgeoisie and that it has none of its own to realize. His critique of liberal republicanism was predicated on the impossibility of actualizing its enlightenment ideals of liberty, equality, and fraternity within the parameters of the capitalist state.

With the triumph of fascism, the degeneration of communism, and the integration of social democracy, these ideals were seen as having lost their cachet and, as a consequence, this kind of political critique as having lost its appeal. Auschwitz had punctured the aura associated with progress and modernity. Old-fashioned criteria for making judgments, constructing narratives, and understanding reality thus become anachronistic. The postmodern appears *avant la lettre*. Enlightenment and modernity find their fulfillment in a concentration camp universe run by an unaccountable bureaucracy, fueled by an instrumental rationality run amok, and expressed in the unleashing of an unimaginable rage.

Dialectic of Enlightenment included fragments of a sensational last chapter "Elements of Anti-Semitism," added in 1947. Prejudice is interpreted there as having its own dynamic and a logic resistant to rational argumentation. Anti-Semitism is viewed as an expression of humanity's "second nature" with anthropological roots. Horkheimer and Adorno insist that there has always been something "different" about the Jews. If modernity is increasingly and repressively standardizing individuality, then the encounter with difference and autonomy will logically generate a resentment born of unconscious envy. Such resentment marks the anti-Semite. Nazi hatred of the Jew fulfills the presentiments of the past even as it produces a "turning point in history."

Capitalism also fits into the picture. Anti-Semitism is not reduced to some prefabricated economic interest. But it is linked to the commodity form through which people are no longer seen as ends unto themselves. They are rather treated as factors of production within a bureaucratic production process. Reification is, meanwhile, undermining the capacity of individuals to exercise moral judgment. Autonomy was being eroded long before the first concentration camp was constructed. The other was always in danger. The Jew was always identified with the sphere of circulation and as the harbinger of capitalism. Not merely capitalism requires interrogation, therefore, but civilization itself. Thus, the critical theory of society takes an anthropological form in which resistance relies upon an increasingly imperiled subjectivity.

Dialectic of Enlightenment insisted that civilization itself was implicated in the assault on subjectivity. Homer's *Odyssey* already depicts the willingness of its main character to surrender his identity and his name in order to survive. Instrumental reason and the erosion of subjectivity, alienation, are thereby intrinsically bound together. The linkage between them is merely crystallized during the historical epoch popularly known as the Enlightenment. The term thus receives a dual meaning in *Dialectic of Enlightenment.* It is identified with both a historically specific scientific theory of knowledge that contested religious dogma in Europe during the seventeenth and eighteenth centuries and, more broadly, an anthropological struggle with error and superstition that arose from the beginnings of civilization. The key to the book is the way in which the historical critique of the Enlightenment is turned into the lever for an anthropological interrogation of progress. This, indeed, is what made it so provocative and controversial.

Objective and value free, operational and testable, scientific reason was initially employed to destroy traditional superstitions and prejudices in order to foster an open discourse, experimentation, and tolerance. Progressive thinkers living in a religious universe were primarily concerned with protecting scientific inquiry from the intrusions of theologians. Having begun with an assault on religious dogmatism, however, instrumental rationality turned its power against all nonscientific precepts and normative claims. These included ethical values associated with the Enlightenment (like moral autonomy and the exercise of conscience) that had inspired scientific experimentation in the first place. Just to this extent, however, the critical character of reason diminished: ever more surely it became, as David Hume had predicted, a "slave of the passions."

Dialectic of Enlightenment supplements Hegel and Marx with insights drawn from Nietzsche, Freud, and Max Weber. Its authors invert the traditional narrative identifying technological development with progress. They instead connect the growing dominance of instrumental rationality with the totally administered society. The new outlook projects a new form of resistance that calls for heightening the "non-identity" between subject and object—or, less philosophically, the individual and society. Insofar as the whole is false, and progress is an illusion, the only critical option lies in developing what would later become known as a negative dialectic. Only in this way might critique confront the illusions attendant upon Enlightenment.

Science had always been treated as value free and neutral regarding ideological claims. Like the commodity form and bureaucracy, however, it has an interest in expanding its dominion. Scientific rationality thus blends easily with the imperatives of capitalism and the bureaucratic state. Capitalism, bureaucracy, and science—all expressions of instrumental rationality—constitute the real core of Enlightenment. They turn nature into an object of use, progress into alienation, and freedom into control. Autonomy is a nuisance and critique is a threat. Enlightenment may be associated with such ideals. But its real goal is standardization and control. In the name of liberation, its advocates wound up fostering a rationality of technical domination. The irrational beliefs that the Enlightenment originally sought to destroy thus reappeared as its own products.

Humanity pays for an increase in power over nature with the loss of subjectivity. Blind to the domination in which it was engaged, equally blind to the reaction it was nurturing, Enlightenment humanism was incapable of understanding that in its "innermost recesses there rages a frantic prisoner who, as a fascist, turns the world into a prison." Such is the real (if unacknowledged) legacy of the Enlightenment. It extends from Kant over the Marquis de Sade to Nietzsche. Where Kant created an epistemological barricade to protect science from the intrusion of metaphysics and religion, and Sade took the instrumental treatment of individuals to the extreme, Nietzsche ultimately rendered reason and conscience subordinate to the will to power.

Dialectic of Enlightenment does not claim that individuals have simply been turned into robots. What occurs instead is a perversion of autonomy. Individuals are seen as increasingly incapable of making anything other than technical or emotional judgments. (Here, it should be noted, the early critique of vulgar materialism and intuitive metaphysics comes into play.) Exercising conscience and imagining the free society become ever more difficult and, if only for this reason, the appeal of totalitarianism grows. A sociological and philosophical explanation—if not a justification—emerges for those who claimed that they were "just following orders." Old-fashioned political forms of resistance are no longer viable: where reification defines progress, critical theory is indeed left in the position of tossing bottles with messages of liberation into the flood of barbarism.

Freedom was betrayed by the Russian revolution, and liberalism compromised the promise of a liberal society. Instrumental rationality saw to that—irrevocably. Philosophical idealism had initially been predicated on the idea of a universal subject lacking all empirical determinants: it was the referent that individuals should use in making ethical decisions. Liberalism employed universal principles for its rule of law and its view on rights. But that is precisely the problem. From the willing surrender of individuality in the name of instrumental needs to the denial of class claims in the name of an abstract humanity to the final assault on metaphysical abstraction itself—all become logical steps within a single logic. Progress is not what the good bourgeois has always said it was: the growth of moral conscience and the improvement of humanity. Quite the opposite: autonomy and ethical norms get obliterated. Actual progress is a movement from the bow and arrow, as Adorno later liked to say, to the atom bomb.

Enlightenment political thought is seen by Horkheimer and Adorno as having bought into the illusion of progress—at great cost. Western Marxists had never been enthralled with liberal republicanism, and in 1933, following the triumph of Adolf Hitler, the Frankfurt School felt the same way. Even Marcuse, perhaps the most politically savvy of its inner circle, noted in 1934 that a deep affinity existed between liberalism and totalitarianism not merely in terms of their commitment to private property but in their political views.

Dialectic of Enlightenment drove home that point. Its authors considered liberalism, while fine as an idea, an apologia for existing conditions. Its blindness to inhumanity and the irrational made liberalism and its humanist impulses, at best, incapable of effectively challenging its enemies and, at worst, complicit with them. They put the matter bluntly: "Enlightenment behaves toward things as a dictator toward men. He knows them insofar as he can manipulate them." Goethe's beloved oak tree sitting in the middle of the Buchenwald concentration camp provides a poignant and symbolic case in point for the fate of Enlightenment.

Horkheimer and Adorno were not merely concerned with the empirical fact that totalitarianism had grown out of a liberal regime like the Weimar Republic. They were convinced that fascism was the product of conditions that existed prior to its triumph not in some negative sense, but as an actual continuation of those conditions it publicly (and hypocritically) denounced. Liberal ideas were betrayed by the instrumental framework in which they were embedded. Its subversion of conscience was made

5. Fascism finds its roots in the Enlightenment. This photograph shows Goethe's beloved oak tree in the Buchenwald concentration camp.

all the worse by the ideals supposedly justifying its existence. The Jew suffered the most: anthropologically because civilization always branded him as "alien" and historically because he was popularly considered the harbinger of liberalism and capitalism.

The irony is unavoidable. Hiding behind the veneer of liberal ideals, the reification process emancipated irrational fears and instinctive drives from the snares of conscience. The resulting anti-Semitism reflects a situation in which "blinded men robbed of their subjectivity are set loose as subjects." There is no reasoning with these hollow individuals. Their irrationalism runs too deep. It was shaped not simply by fascism but by civilization and the unintended consequences of the enlightenment legacy.

The retreat from history

In his "Theses on the Philosophy of History," Walter Benjamin noted that there is "no document of civilization that is not at the same time a document of barbarism." Perhaps. But this claim only begs the question: how to differentiate between the two and determine which quality is more prevalent in any given work. *Dialectic of Enlightenment* never articulated the criteria necessary for providing an answer. Its authors refused to deal with the Enlightenment in terms of its influence upon institutions, movements, and political ideals. They identified it instead with a single form of rationality and then interrogated that in terms of a single anthropological narrative. The Enlightenment is taken to task without reference to the Counter-Enlightenment. The historical conflicts over constraining the arbitrary exercise of institutional power, and fostering the free exercise of individuality, simply vanish. Intellectual traditions lose their relation to organized forms of practice. There is only instrumental rationality: the transformative agent or, better, the new world spirit.

Dialectic of Enlightenment never treats the seminal political thinkers. There is hardly a word about John Locke, Gotthold

Lessing, Voltaire, Benjamin Franklin, or Tom Paine. The book's authors looked farther. Their concern was with the Marquis de Sade, Schopenhauer, Bergson, and Nietzsche. Not one of them identified either with Enlightenment political principles or the organizations dedicated to realizing them. They were anti-liberal, anti-socialist, anti-democratic and anti-egalitarian, anti-rationalist and anti-historical.

Horkheimer and Adorno's critique of scientific rationality is also politically misleading. Fascists were never infatuated with scientific rationality or universal categories. They instead made ideological use of notions like "Jewish physics" or "Italian mathematics." Most positivist and neo-positivist exponents of scientific rationality in the twentieth century were liberals like Karl Popper; some were social democrats like Rudolf Carnap; and a few like Hans Reichenbach were even once members of the ultra-Left. Norberto Bobbio, the great socialist thinker and activist, was surely correct when he noted that contempt for positivism (not its embrace) was a hallmark of fascism.

None of this, apparently, was relevant. Horkheimer and Adorno were more interested in the dialectical process that works behind the conscious intentions of individuals and groups. But their dialectic lacked historical specification. They never inquired into the moments of *political* decision that produced the new barbarism. *Dialectic of Enlightenment* has nothing to say about the Dreyfus Affair, the Russian Revolution, the fascist March on Rome, or the Nazi triumph. The organizational and ideological conflicts remain as invisible as the personalities involved. The connection between totalitarianism and modernity—with the Enlightenment as its source and instrumental rationality as its medium—simply doesn't wash.

It remains unclear why the most advanced capitalist nations like the United States and England never experienced a genuine fascist threat while far less advanced nations, like Italy and

Romania, succumbed to the forces of reaction. It is also unclear why Japan never experienced the Enlightenment. Nor is there a discussion of totalitarianism from the Left. What occurred in the Soviet Union was a product not of modernity but the lack of it: Gramsci actually considered the Bolshevik revolution "a revolution against *Das Kapital*" while Leon Trotsky and Lenin maintained that the communist triumph was possible only because Imperial Russia was "the weakest link in the capitalist chain."

Orthodox Marxists among the social democratic leadership—not surprisingly—were clearer about all this than the far more philosophically sophisticated members of the Frankfurt School. Karl Kautsky and Rosa Luxemburg not only predicted the emergence of a terror apparatus in the Soviet Union as early as 1918, but analyzed it as the product of economic underdevelopment. Other scholars would note that in Germany the bourgeoisie had not yet ideologically come to terms with feudalism when fear of the proletariat led to its alignment with the reaction.

European fascism was *not* the product of some prefabricated philosophical dialectic but rather the self-conscious ideological response to liberalism and social democracy. Its mass base everywhere lay primarily in pre-capitalist classes—the peasantry, the underclass, and the petite-bourgeoisie—whose existential and material interests seemed threatened by the capitalist production process and its two dominant classes: the bourgeoisie and the proletariat. Classes identified with modernity mostly supported political parties embracing a continental form of liberalism or a social democratic party still formally embracing orthodox Marxism and its communist rival. All these parties except the communists were supporters of the Weimar Republic, and all were enemies of the Nazis who made war on them in word and deed.

Dialectic of Enlightenment casts these real historical conflicts into a metaphysical fog. Its famous interpretation of Odysseus, whose denial of his identity becomes the only way for him to survive his exile, offers a case in point. "The sacrifice of consciousness is carried out according to its own categories, rationally." There is no turning back. Instrumental reason is necessary to survive and the forms in which we survive generate our destruction. Enlightenment is the story of a dynamic whose reifying effects culminate in the number tattooed on the arm of a concentration camp inmate. There is an extraordinary sweep to this provocative argument. But it is predicated on false concreteness and misplaced causality. Instrumental reason did not bring about Nazism or even destroy the ability of individuals to make normative judgments. The Nazi victory was rather the product of a clash between real movements whose members were quite capable of making diverse judgments concerning both their interests and their values.

Fascism was never a foregone conclusion just as it was never simply a function of modernity. Real movements and real organizations, real traditions and real ideas, were in conflict. To ignore them is to embrace the reification of thinking that the Frankfurt School nominally sought to oppose. What emerges from *Dialectic of Enlightenment* is an unyielding process that excludes more than it illuminates—precisely because it is neither determinate in its historical claims nor precise in its political judgments. The desire to unify qualitatively different phenomena under a single rubric could only produce historical disorientation and political confusion. Given his own association with Stalinism, Lukács may not have been one to point fingers. Nevertheless, there is something legitimate about his quip that the Frankfurt School watched the descent into barbarism from its "grand hotel abyss."

What next?

Max Horkheimer and Theodor W. Adorno intended to confront the limits of Enlightenment from the standpoint of enlightenment itself. Their point of departure was the erosion of autonomy. Progress is seen by them as generating barbarism and the critique of capitalism is situated within a broader "anthropology of domination." Their undertaking stands squarely within the dialectical tradition of Marxism. But the positive moment underpinning their critique never becomes concrete or clear. Because the whole is false, and mediations are never introduced, critical theory becomes compelled to consider negation as its guiding principle. The totally administered society is a product of teleology in reverse. Reification is creeping into every crevice of society and instrumental rationality, wherever it appears, is evincing yet another form of domination. Horkheimer and Adorno provide no criteria for drawing distinctions. For them, the basic situation is obvious: instrumental rationality is the problem, the commodity form is the culprit, and the culture industry is the enemy. There is no alternative. There is only an ongoing resistance waged in the name of an always elusive, if supposedly genuine, experience of individuality.

Dialectic of Enlightenment was intended to have a sequel. Its authors might have felt that they had gone too far. Horkheimer had hopes for a "positive dialectical doctrine which has not yet been written." The Enlightenment seemed to require rescuing or reclaiming. But that never came to fruition. There is much debate regarding why not. Some look to the fragmentary organization of the work—its use of aphorisms, montage, and its anti-systemic character. Others highlight the authors' intellectual investment in negation. Still others point to their break with the Left and their fear of political engagement. Yet, there might be a different reason. Its authors might simply have found it impossible to offer a "positive dialectical doctrine"—because they no longer had anything "positive" to say.

Chapter 5
The utopian laboratory

In 1795, Friedrich Schiller published his *Letters on the Aesthetic Education of Man*. His aim was to preserve the utopian promises that the French Revolution had destroyed in the terror and the subsequent conservative swing—or Thermidor—that followed the execution of Robespierre in 1793. Schiller introduced aesthetics as a utopian response to reality. His classic work describes a new life-world in which the play impulse with its sensuous and form-giving qualities transforms existence and, implicitly, redefines the character of labor and science. The aesthetic realm incarnates the "inner truth" of humanity. Obliterating differences of status and power, it projects new forms of solidarity, freedom, and a non-instrumental treatment of nature. Utopia inheres within the "beautiful illusion" generated by art. But this illusion also serves as a regulative ideal. It shapes reality in accord with its own liberating standards and purposes: it embodies the promise of happiness that history has betrayed.

The Frankfurt School would experiment with redeeming the ruins, fragments, and forgotten images that point to the realization of that promise. The proletarian revolution of its time may have turned totalitarian and the new vanguard may have failed in its historical mission. But, still, the reclamation project of the Frankfurt School bore a Marxian stamp. New material conditions were seen as justifying its turn to aesthetics and metaphysics. Contesting the totally administered society and the domination of instrumental reason called for rejecting the usual attempts to employ art for political purposes.

A critical standpoint on aesthetics now suggested that the aim of art is not to depict the wrongs of society in realistic terms, offer platitudes about how things should be, or pander to the masses. Critical theory must redefine mimesis with an eye on montage, stream of consciousness, and other techniques that offer new forms—new illusions—for experiencing reality and eliciting the utopian longings of the audience. These longings are probably strongest when the conditions for their realization are most improbable. Herein perhaps is the meaning behind the famous words of Walter Benjamin from his essay on Goethe: "It is only for the sake of the hopeless that hope is given to us."

Anticipating utopia

Ernst Bloch liked to quote those words. But he believed that utopia requires a more robust political and philosophical underpinning—and he sought to provide just that in his lifelong preoccupation with the "dream of the better life." Attempts to demonstrate its content led to disquisitions on everything from reincarnation to alchemy. But he also offered a material foundation for utopia in the failed uprisings, forgotten experiments, and unrealized ideas that comprise the underground history of the revolution. All of them provide intimations of a world built on equality, justice, and freedom. Bloch's writings thus reinvigorate an idea old as humanity itself. Their unfinished, free-flowing, and associative character complements their classical erudition, expressionist literary style, and apocalyptic visions. Anticipatory fantasy mixes with a critical use of memory. Impulses for political emancipation are gleaned from the workers' councils of his time back over to the free towns of Europe, the theology of forgotten Protestant revolutionaries like Thomas Munzer, the origins of natural right, and the sacred texts of the most varied religions.

Admittedly: the claims made by Bloch were too often asserted rather than argued; his interpretive criteria were sometimes vague; and he often blurred the line between fantasy and logic. Yet, his desire was to make utopia concrete. The best life contests every currently alienated moment of the totality. It projects a unity between subject and object that turns the world into an experiment for the most diverse practices of individuality. The purpose animating this vast enterprise crystallizes in the closing lines of Bloch's three-volume *The Principle of Hope*:

> . . . . man everywhere is still living in prehistory, indeed all and everything still stands before the creation of the world, of a right world. True genesis is not at the beginning but at the end, and it starts to begin only when society and existence become radical, i.e., grasp their roots. But the root of history is the working, creating human being who reshapes and overhauls the given facts. Once he has grasped himself and re-established what is his, without expropriation and alienation, in real democracy, there arises in the world something which shines into the childhood of all and in which no one has yet been: a homeland.

Ernst Bloch subscribed to a version of this position throughout his long life. His *Subject-Object* (1949) and the famous conclusion to *Spirit of Utopia* (1918), "Karl Marx, Death and the Apocalypse," evince roughly the same vision. A mainstay of the German avant-garde, a maverick Marxist who ultimately endorsed Stalinism in the 1930s, Bloch became a professor at the University of Leipzig after World War II, emigrated to the West when the Berlin Wall was erected in 1961, and taught at the University of Tübingen until his death. In the years before World War I, he and Lukács were best friends. They became Marxists together, and their work reflected the ambitions and hopes associated with the heroic years of the Russian Revolution. They were always together in the cafes and attending events—so much so that elements of both were fused into the character of Naphta, the intolerant authoritarian with Jesuitical traits, in the great prewar novel *The Magic Mountain* by Thomas Mann. The two friends broke over various aesthetic and philosophical matters in the late 1920s. Nevertheless, the rift between them only became public during the 1930s in an exchange over the political implications of literature that became known as "the expressionism debate."

Lukács had made his peace with the Communist International following its condemnation of *History and Class Consciousness* in 1924. He resolved to remain within the organization, and he kept to that resolution. His thinking became more rigid and more doctrinaire yet, for better or worse, also more concerned with linking the revolutionary heritage of the bourgeoisie with communism. That certainly served as his motivation for initiating what undoubtedly became the most important literary debate of the interwar period.

Echoing the growing call for an anti-fascist Popular Front, trying to understand the cultural roots of Nazism, Lukács challenged European modernism in general and German expressionism in particular for their irrationalism, subjectivism, and utopianism. Essays like "Greatness and Decline of Expressionism" (1934) and "Realism in the Balance" (1938) maintain that fashionable avant-garde trends helped create the cultural preconditions in which fascism could thrive. Lukács' alternative was a form of "critical realism" perhaps best exemplified in the works of Honore de Balzac, Leo Tolstoy, and Thomas Mann.

In "Discussing Expressionism" (1938) and other essays, Bloch took issue with Lukács' line of reasoning. He opposed reducing literature to politics, insisted upon the humanitarian character of the expressionist enterprise, and highlighted its assault upon the cultural philistinism that was so much a part of the fascist worldview. Bloch also defended expressionism for its utopian sensibility and its vision of the new man. He never renounced his early writings. In contrast to Lukács, who once claimed that the worst form of socialism is better than the best form of capitalism, Bloch always contended that the worst form of socialism is not socialism at all. Socialism must prefigure the best life if it is to prove worthy of its name. Utopia cannot remain the land that Samuel Butler called *erewhon*—or nowhere (sort of) spelled backwards.

Bloch understood socialism as a projection of utopia. It should serve as a reconfigured totality that provides new ways of treating humanity and nature as well as new opportunities for experiencing the richness of civilization. His outlook was eschatological, but it was never reducible to faith or symbols. Utopian anticipations can be found in the most basic human experiences and images that hark back to the garden of Eden. But the best also becomes manifest in the thrill of sports, the desire for love, nursery rhymes, daydreams, and the lightness experienced in a genuine work of art. Each is a dim prefiguration of the world we

6. The Garden of Eden is perhaps the most powerful image of utopia.

seek, and human history is one long struggle in the multiple dimensions of life to articulate and realize it.

Underpinning all our disappointments and fears, including death, is the hope for redemption and the freedom that has been denied humanity. Utopia receives an ontological foundation in the experience of hope and the inherently incomplete character of existence. The task of critical thinking is to illuminate these unconscious and half-conscious yearnings by highlighting the "anticipatory consciousness" that allows for reinterpreting the past. Bloch's *Atheism in Christianity* (1968), for example, emphasizes the religious roots of communism; it would serve to influence liberation theology that became so popular in Latin America and elsewhere in the former colonized world. *Natural Law and Human Dignity* (1961), meanwhile, insists that the hope for equitable treatment and the constraint of arbitrary institutional power has always animated the strivings of the lowly and the insulted.

Utopia makes us aware that what we have is not necessarily what we want and that what we want is not necessarily all we can have. Enlightenment thinking becomes open to criticism—according to Bloch—insofar as it reduces the rational to the real, and it remains blind to the unrealized utopian elements buried in magic, madness, childhood fantasies, and the like. Arguments can be made that he romanticized these states of mind, overidentified with those who laud them, and overestimated their salience for utopian philosophy. But the critical moment of Bloch's enterprise is an attempt—one that stands squarely within the tradition of critical theory—to illuminate the *ratio of the irratio*. This is of importance not simply for making sense of magic and mysticism but for understanding the "false utopias" embedded in racism and other ideologies that privilege the intuitive and the irrational.

Bloch always maintained that the future is not some mechanical elaboration of the present. It does not emerge from a series of steps or stages that lead into the future by obliterating the past. At the same time, however, utopia should not be considered as an abrupt break with reality. In dialectical fashion, instead, utopia constitutes a specific and renewal of the past that renders conscious what exists but is not yet conscious. Every story is thereby open to interpretation and the interpretation to reinterpretation. Existence is always unfinished—its end is always "not yet" in sight. There is no absolute salvation or redemption. There is no Day of Judgment. The dream of the best life constantly glimmers anew as humanity reflects on what it has ignored.

Artifacts from every corner of the earth and previously unacknowledged treasures evince the incomplete dream of the best life. Bloch's gaze wanders from Zoroaster and Confucius to legendary stories of the fictional Scheherazade and the sixteenth-century prophecies of Nostradamus to Romanticism, Marxism, and Modernism. Different understandings of time, death, kindness, and the most varied sentiments come to life in what Bloch termed the "utopian laboratory." Tolerance and a cosmopolitan mind-set are essential for its functioning. All the more sad, and ironic, that Bloch should have defended the show trials scripted by Joseph Stalin in a notorious 1938 essay titled "Jubilee for Renegades". No other thinker has ever produced a utopian conception as rich, varied, fresh, and pregnant with possibilities. There is hope for transforming every moment of the totality. But the whole is more than the sum of its parts, and attempts to realize the anticipatory potential of one element will inevitably impinge upon another. What Bloch termed "the world experiment" is incapable of being fully redeemed: utopia must always remain utopian.

The pacification of existence

Herbert Marcuse agreed. But the way in which he dealt with utopia was very different. His *Eros and Civilization* (1955) is an attempt to articulate the liberating desires, hopes, and fantasies that have been repressed since time immemorial. Marcuse had been interested in Schiller since the beginnings of his intellectual career. Young radicals of his generation embraced him far more than Goethe or the rest of the eighteenth-century Weimar literati. After Auschwitz and the Gulag, and the prospect of nuclear annihilation in a new cold war, Marcuse saw the need for a new vantage point from which critique might be launched. The beautiful illusion, the play impulse, and the idea of sustained happiness provided the fitting basis for an anthropological break with the reality principle and, its capitalist variant, the performance principle.

Freud had associated these terms with delayed gratification of pleasure and the repression of instinctual sexual desires lodged in the unconscious. All this was deemed necessary in order to survive in a world of scarcity. Marcuse suggested, however, that the modern world of scarcity was being artificially maintained. A kind of "surplus repression" was being enforced by the structure of advanced industrial society to assure its continuation.

Imperialism, militarism, economic exploitation, patriarchal family structures, religious dogmatism, and the false needs generated by consumerism all render it irrational. Only a kind of primal guilt maintains the identification with its values and institutions. Punishment is sought and employed to quell the desire for liberation and archetypical thoughts of rebellion by the sons against the unequal distribution of work and satisfaction imposed by the primal father. Too terrible to recall, shrouded in mist, these rebellions and vague dreams of liberation must be expunged. Deadened by the culture industry, bereft of alternatives, lacking in reflexivity, caught within the whirl of a fast-paced yet ultimately meaningless existence, individuals thus lose control of their history.

Insofar as repression fosters irrational resentments and violence, social and political activity focuses ever less upon liberation than destruction. But this only further intensifies the utopian longings along with guilt and the subsequent need for new punishments based on ever more manipulative and unnecessary methods of delaying gratification. Material progress thus rests on psychological regression. Unable to deal with their guilt, the individuals living in advanced industrial society constantly reproduce the repressive values of the performance principle.

Utopia is the denial of all this. It projects sublimated forms of creative activity that bind subject and object, and that free the libido from all constraints. Humanity is psychologically reconfigured in utopia. Scarcity is overcome, and individuals cease to view one another in instrumental terms. People are placed before profits, work turns into play, and a new sensibility takes shape that is almost biologically repulsed by cruelty, exploitation, and violence. And that is not all. Time is no longer conceived in linear terms but rather, following nature, as an internal circular process akin to what Nietzsche termed the "eternal recurrence." Sustained happiness thus finally becomes a speculative possibility in the thought that death is not the unfolding of life. *An Essay on Liberation* becomes the vehicle for Marcuse to depict a utopian existence in which:

> techniques would then tend to become art, and art would tend to form reality: the opposition between imagination and reason, higher and lower faculties, poetic and scientific thought, would be invalidated. Emergence of a new Reality Principle: under which a new sensibility and a de-sublimated scientific intelligence would combine in the creation of an aesthetic ethos.

Eros and Civilization in particular has generated an avalanche of criticism. But it remains an imaginative tour de force. That work transformed the deeply pessimistic outlook of Freud in *Civilization and Its Discontents* (1930) and his other metapsychological speculations into the foundation for a radically utopian vision. Anchoring the desire for restructuring the instincts, intent upon challenging alienation in the most dramatic way, Marcuse offers a liberating counterpoint to the sadistic perversion of human nature in the concentration camp universe. He insists that only the "pacification of existence," a sustained experience of happiness without fear of death, can bring about the triumph of Eros over Thanatos. Utopia is the only viable standpoint for confronting a world in which progress is actually an expression of barbarism.

Eros and Civilization was published at a time when intellectual life in the Western world was dominated by Jean-Paul Sartre and the Existentialists in France, Günther Grass and the "Group '47" in Germany, and the Beats in the United States. Marcuse offered something different. His vision contested their pessimism and, later, challenged young people to broaden their minds and embrace ethical idealism of a new sort. Marcuse was no fool. He knew that his utopia was predicated on a contradiction that prevented its realization: only already liberated individuals can bring about a liberated society. He was also aware that his vision was speculative in character and critical for precisely that reason. But some believed that his ideas constituted a threat to the rational foundations of critical theory.

Jürgen Habermas's "Technology and Science as 'Ideology'" (1968) offers a devastating attack on Marcuse and a very different point of view. His claim is that technology has an ontological structure and that talk of a new science is illegitimate without articulating criteria for verifying truth claims. A counterargument would suggest, however, that such criticisms are external rather than immanent. They don't speak to what is at stake. The real issue is whether *Eros and Civilization* offers an appropriately ideal standard to indict reality. Or, more bluntly, how genuinely utopian is its vision and how radical are its implications?

Erich Fromm undertakes his criticism of Marcuse with just these questions in mind. His arguments appear in various essays collected in *The Crisis of Psychoanalysis* (1970) and *The Revision of Psychoanalysis* (1992). Highlighting the primacy of social conditions on character formation, Fromm had already questioned Freud's metapsychological claims and instinct theory during the 1930s. This estranged him from the inner circle of the Institute for Social Research and led, in 1939, to his formal severance from it. As far as Fromm was concerned any philosophical grounding for psychology, or metapsychology, is useful only insofar as it is linked to clinical practice. Without connection to the real experiences of real individuals, such a metapsychology will necessarily rely on an arbitrary manipulation of concepts and ignore the problems associated with alleviating personal suffering. Fromm points to various technical mistakes made by Marcuse.

Polymorphous sexuality, for example, is defined by Freud in terms of prepubescent sexuality so that the supposedly utopian longing for its fulfillment (claimed by Marcuse) is actually predicated on infantile fantasies. *Eros and Civilization* is thus seen by Fromm as forwarding a notion of utopia that actually serves as a veil for regression and the obliteration of the ego. Even if this were not the case, however, critical theory should still emphasize the primacy of therapeutic attempts to foster the maturity, independence, and rationality of individuals in capitalist society. Any other position, whatever its utopian claims, severs theory from practice and speculative claims from empirical validation—thereby betraying the original vision and rational character of the critical enterprise.

Former associates within the inner circle took all this very seriously. They believed that Fromm's assault on metapsychology constituted a revision of Freud's radical legacy. It threatened to obliterate the legitimacy of engaging in the kind of anthropological critique of civilization that inspired *Dialectic of the Enlightenment*. Theodor W. Adorno subjected Fromm's views to fierce criticism in "Social Science and Sociological Tendencies in Psychoanalysis" (1946). Marcuse also counterattacked with a criticism of Freudian "revisionism" that first appeared in the pages of *Dissent* (1956) and ultimately served as the appendix to *Eros and Civilization*. Important issues are involved here that speak to the character of critical theory and the direction it should take.

If Fromm is correct, then critical theory must again—though in new ways and under new conditions—view itself as a theory of practice. It should offer practical ideas for dealing with exploitation and repression, and rely more strongly on the ethical traditions associated with humanism and the Enlightenment. Embracing metapsychology, by contrast, affirms the ontology of false conditions. Only negative dialectics and visions of an anthropological break can then preserve the possibility of resistance and the radical idea of freedom. Theory trumps practice. Privileging clinical therapy to better the psychological plight of individuals becomes a form of compromise with the status quo and an adaptation to repression. Adorno put the matter strikingly in *Minima Moralia*: "Wrong life cannot be lived rightly." But then: it's also possible that the wrong life can be more or less wrong, and living it can occur more or less rightly.

What's missing?

The Frankfurt School offered understandings of the best life very different than those provided in *Utopia* (1516) by Thomas More or the American best seller *Looking Backward* (1887), by Edward Bellamy. These classics of utopian literature integrated standard assumptions of the world they sought to contest like slavery or technological progress. Works that envision an anthropological or even a genuinely radical break with the reality principle are rare. The dangers implicit in that idea actually constitute a fundamental theme of dis-utopian works like *We* (1921) by Yevgeny Zamyatin, *Brave New World* (1932) by Aldous Huxley, or *Animal Farm* (1945) and *1984* (1949) by George Orwell. All of them provide a trenchant critique of communist totalitarianism and technological progress. They also warn against moral libertinism and the vision of sustained happiness. Utopia—or, better, the dream of realizing it—is treated by them as a seductive narcotic with a special set of dangers.

Perhaps that is as it should be. Attempts to turn utopia into reality had bloody results long before communism and fascism entered the historical scene. The idea of apocalyptic redemption forecloses compromise. Utopia has always been laden with the self-righteousness born of prophecy—and, as often as not, the celebration of violence. Utopians traditionally justified the terrible means they employed by the liberating ends they supposedly guaranteed. There is ample reason for deriding utopia as irrational and abstract, vague and indeterminate, oblivious of human nature.

But the dream of the best life is an enduring theme of humanity. Utopia might be the most underestimated concept in the philosophical lexicon. It also has exceptional practical importance. Every mass ideology has a utopian component. The great movements were never inspired, and the barricades never mounted for purely pragmatic reasons. "Man does not live by bread alone," Bloch wrote, "especially when he doesn't have any." Utopia has an existential component: it is the ideal for which countless individuals have proven willing to die.

Theorists should remain wary of depicting utopia too realistically. But there is always room for a sketch that can be retouched and redrawn. The sketch provides little more than the outlines for what will always remain an unfinished painting. Utopia is ultimately a regulative ideal: it provides us with a sense of how little civilization has achieved and anticipatory traces of what might be achieved in the future. Utopia has inspired revolutions. But it has also inspired the arduous, boring, and sometimes dangerous efforts at reform. Even therapeutic attempts to better the lives of individuals make reference to ideas and ideals concerning how life should be lived. Utopia need not make political actors blind to social reality and ethical constraints.

The sketch can clarify the multifaceted problems attendant upon furthering the best life. It can also show how humanity is still a work in process. Utopia was never meant to obliterate the individual. Better to view it as privileging a "multiplicity in unity" and fostering a richer and more complex form of individuality.

The best life escapes being captured by images, circumscribed by depictions, and reduced to philosophical categories. That is its strength. Utopia exposes how reality exists under what T. W. Adorno termed the "wicked spell"—the fetish surrounding immediate gratification that erodes the critical imagination. Perhaps utopia does only exist in the moment when one is lying on one's back in the grass looking at the sky, freed of want and pressure like Ferdinand the Baby Bull, the hero of children's books, or in the flash of time that departs as soon as it is experienced. But, then, utopia does not rest on a single longing or a single desire—even the longing for immorality or the desire for sustained happiness and ultimate meaning. The truly subversive idea in Brecht's utopian play *Mahagonny* (1929) was that "something is missing"—but then something is always missing.

Chapter 6
The happy consciousness

Hegel believed that progress is ultimately furthered by the person who is out of step with the majority. Only this person, the genuine nonconformist, really experiences the constraints on freedom. Only this person is in the position of questioning the prevailing understandings of happiness. For Hegel, indeed, the "unhappy consciousness" is the source of progress. That is also the case for the Frankfurt School. Its members posed many criticisms of modern life and the culture industry. But the danger that advanced industrial society presents to the unhappy consciousness is perhaps the most telling. At stake is the substance of subjectivity and autonomy: the will and ability of the individual to resist external forces intent upon determining the meaning and experience of life.

Max Horkheimer wrote to Leo Lowenthal that mass culture was cheating the individual out of his own experience of time, or what Henri Bergson called the *durée*. Marcuse feared that people no longer had the capacity to act as subjects and that they were being manipulated into thinking that something depended on their choices. Horkheimer and Adorno articulated what would become the general stance of the inner circle in *Dialectic of Enlightenment*:

> Life in the late capitalist era is a constant initiation rite. Everyone must show that he wholly identifies himself with the power which is

7. Conformism and loss of individuality mark the happy consciousness.

belaboring him. This occurs in the principle of jazz syncopation, which simultaneously derides stumbling and makes it a rule. The eunuch-like voice of the crooner on the radio, the heiress's smooth suitor, who falls into the swimming pool in his dinner jacket, are models for those who must become whatever the system wants. Everyone can be like this omnipotent society; everyone can be happy, if only he will capitulate fully and sacrifice his claim to happiness.

Writing as a young rebel about other young rebels, caught between disgust for an old culture and longing for the new, Georg *von* Lukács—he employed the aristocratic designation at the time—envisioned a transformative role for the critic in *Soul and Form* (1911). Its literary and philosophical essays were evocative, complex, esoteric, and decidedly nontraditional. Art enabled the individual to resist society not simply by challenging popular tastes and perceptions, or so Lukács argued, but by intensifying experience through its allegorical and symbolic qualities.

Critical interpretation might prove necessary in order to elicit them. In turn, however, such philosophical interrogation would generate other interpretations. Both the philosophical exercise in literary criticism and the work of art are thus unfinished by definition. They are always open to reinterpretation by new audiences at new times. That is because products of creative activity harbor a secret to be uncovered and then recovered. No less than the artwork, the critical essay through its form can elicit repressed experiences of the soul. The boundaries between philosophy and aesthetics, reflection and experience, start to collapse. The artist in Lukács's new and broader definition of the term now appears as a "problematical man." Not the political revolutionary but the erudite cultural radical with a bohemian bent—like Nietzsche—is the agent of the new: the prophet of an invigorated subjectivity, an emergent culture, and a transformed reality.

How the culture industry works

The Frankfurt School assumed that opposition to mass society meant opposition to mass culture. Its inner circle took the standpoint of the intellectual outsider. They knew that mass media tends to champion right-wing causes. But they also knew that the culture industry can also produce works of a seemingly progressive slant. Mass media had already often bashed capitalism, intolerance, and the power elite. Even then, however, it seems to standardize experience and undermine critical reflection. According to the Frankfurt School, the culture industry integrates all opposition by its very nature. The impotence of a work is a direct function of its popularity. No work is safe: not the nonobjective paintings of Wassily Kandinsky and not the rigorously intellectual music of Arnold Schönberg.

A dynamic is involved: classical music once served as a backdrop for movies (like those of Charlie Chaplin and Fritz Lang) while today it often serves as the backdrop for commercials. The anti-traditional avant-garde has, meanwhile, entered the museum. Its works, too, can now be contemplated serenely by liberal individuals of good will. Sometimes the cultural philistine will be made to feel a bit uncomfortable by what the culture industry presents. But the fuss is over nothing. The critical or utopian potential within the artwork has already been nullified. It has been reduced to just another form of free expression in a free and affluent society.

The Frankfurt School believed that the culture industry is an essential feature of the totally administered society. Marxists had always viewed culture as a prop for the ruling class, and Louis Althusser later wrote about an "ideological-state-apparatus." But the Frankfurt School took this line of argument in a different direction. Assumptions made by the inner circle concerning the character of mass culture, its ongoing assault on intellectual standards, involve the integration of concerns that were first raised by conservatives.

In the eighteenth century, Edmund Burke already fretted that the "fine draperies of life" were being torn asunder, and his less sophisticated and more radical nineteenth- and twentieth-century followers insisted with Gustav Le Bon that "the populace is sovereign and the tide of barbarism mounts." Elites always warned against what Jose Ortega y Gasset called "the mass man" and his entry into public life. All this makes it important to highlight the differences between critical theory and the various assaults on mass culture by genuine reactionaries.

Horkheimer, Adorno, Benjamin, and Marcuse were not unduly worried about the threat to tradition and cultural authority. They were closer to Nietzsche, the cultural revolutionary rather than the political reactionary, who decried Victorian decadence with its puritanical conformism and hypocrisy, its dead materialism and stultifying rationalism. For the Frankfurt School it remained a matter of the "higher spirit" being doomed to misunderstanding or worse by a "herd" incapable of intellectually mastering its "will to power."

If the whole is untrue, if there is no way of affecting society politically, then cultural criticism becomes the only source of resistance. The baton shifts from Hegel and Marx to Nietzsche, whose aristocratic radicalism made him an exponent of high art against its popular rival and of modernism against the cultural philistine. He was a cosmopolitan and opposed the vulgar anti-Semitism embraced by people like the composer Richard Wagner, who often hid his prejudices under the cloak of "nationalism." But Nietzsche was also skeptical of the supposedly universal foundations of morality and science. He had little sympathy for the masses or the democratic ethos embodied in progressive mass movements. Disgusted by what he considered the growing mediocrity of his society, acutely aware of the deepening cultural malaise, and intuiting apocalypse, Nietzsche championed experimentation, individuality, and a "perspectival" view of reality.

Dialectic of Enlightenment took up these themes. But its authors' views on the culture industry were already evinced in earlier works. Adorno's "On the Fetish Character of Music and the Regression of Listening" (1938) noted that the products of the culture industry were not works of art that were only later packaged as commodities but, instead, conceived as commodities from their inception. Horkheimer followed suit by embracing high art as against popular entertainment in "Art and Mass Culture" (1941).

Only the most technically complex works, both of them believed, could foster reflection and resistance against declining cultural standards and perpetually changing fashions. The issue is not the political content but the form in which it is expressed—the medium is the message. Adorno put the matter bluntly in *Minima Moralia*: "the value of a thought is measured by its distance from the continuity of the familiar. It is objectively devalued as this distance is reduced."

The Frankfurt School was elitist in its view of public life. Yet its members were decidedly modernist in their inclinations. They harbored no romantic illusions about some bygone golden age, and they were unconcerned with the existential anxieties of the establishment. They were intent upon challenging the culture industry because it was standardizing experience and thereby rendering everyday people more and more receptive to tradition and authority. Material riches were, in keeping with the old bohemian and romantic idea, seen by the Frankfurt School as impoverishing the spirit. The happy consciousness was condemned because it was hollow and vapid. Herbert Marcuse insisted that the culture industry was complicit in closing the political universe.

Quiescence of the individual and the closure of political life were considered a function of capitalism, the bureaucratic state, and the mass media. Jürgen Habermas analyzed this in his groundbreaking first book, *The Structural Transformation of the Public Sphere* (1961). Its subtitle in German is "a category of bourgeois society." Alexander Kluge and Oskar Negt, two younger students of Adorno, later complemented this enterprise with their own study of its "proletarian" rival. Nevertheless, it was Habermas who introduced the public sphere into the sociological lexicon.

He viewed this realm as mediating between the organized political institutions of the state and the economic forces of civil society. The public sphere included all the activities and organizations capable of fostering public debate. These range from the free press to the town meeting, from the family to salons, and from the educational system to the cheap production of books. The roots of the public sphere may derive from the medieval free cities, but it gained ground during the Enlightenment and the democratic revolutions of 1688–1789. This was the context in which open deliberation became a value in its own right, the aggrieved masses employed their common sense, and individuals exercised their civil rights. Public opinion was a source of empowerment: it tended to protect the individual from the arbitrary power of regimes still wavering between monarchy and republicanism.

All the great movements for political democracy and material equality—from the social democratic labor movement of the nineteenth century to the civil rights movement and the women's liberation movement of the 1960s—generated a vibrant public sphere. It is even fair to say that the character and power of a movement can be gleaned from the vitality of its public sphere.

With respect to empowering the masses, however, the problem arose once public opinion became identified with publicity. As the mass media gained dominance, popular struggles began surrendering their power to the organizations and experts involved with the bureaucratic welfare state. The new cultural apparatus increasingly placed a premium on consensus and narrowed the range of debate. Habermas would remain preoccupied with the role played by democratic will formation throughout his career. There is a reason why he initially embraced the student movement of the 1960s. He also continued to believe that an altered civil society might yet contest the increasing dominance of instrumental reason: *Legitimation Crisis* (1975) remains one of his most salient (if neglected) works. But Habermas's emphasis upon the primacy of the liberating discourse and political participation was not shared by most members of the inner circle. As far as they were concerned, "only the word coined by commerce" holds sway, and attempts at mass enlightenment can only result in mass deception.

Reification maintains its hold over public life. More than that—an ontology of false conditions imperils subjectivity and the ability of individuals to render moral judgments. Resistance against the power of the happy consciousness thus turns into an ethical imperative. At least that is what the Frankfurt School believed. The question is only what such resistance implies and entails. If the totally administered society is truly total, and capable of integrating and domesticating all critical undertakings, then the prospects for political action are dim. Resistance as political practice is a worthless enterprise. The negation is the only available option, and negative dialectics must define the critical enterprise. If organized activity can prove effective, by contrast, then the system is not totally administered and, since meaningful alternatives exist (with respect to policy and programs), a different critical approach is required. Viewing the totally administered society as an immanent tendency doesn't help matters: negative dialectics and a theory of practice are mutually exclusive alternatives.

Tolerance and public life

Following the return of the Institute for Social Research to Germany in 1947, ironically, its inner circle turned into genuine public intellectuals. Max Horkheimer became Rector for the University of Frankfurt. Fearful of both communism and the kind of social disruption that generated Nazism, he supported the Vietnam War and proved a staunch critic of the student movement. Herbert Marcuse and Erich Fromm, meanwhile, became intellectual superstars during the 1960s and 1970s. Both identified with the New Left and openly supported movements concerned with social justice, anti-imperialism, human rights, the abolition of nuclear weapons, and constraints on the military-industrial complex.

As for Jürgen Habermas, his essays on contemporary political matters have been collected in countless volumes. An early advocate of educational reform and the New Left, though sharply critical of its excesses, Habermas always honored its commitments to radical democracy and social justice. Even T. W. Adorno took on a public role. Known as a fierce critic of the New Left, which was often represented by his own radical students, he provided dozens of radio interviews and popular essays that sought to clarify his ideas. He even offered a withering analysis of astrology in "The Stars Down To Earth" (1953).

If the Frankfurt School was participating in the public sphere, of course, it was legitimate to ask whether this did not indicate the existence of an open society. Tolerance was apparently being extended to critics of the totally administered society. That situation might produce conceptual confusion. Herbert Marcuse sought to deal with this matter in what became perhaps his most notorious essay "Repressive Tolerance" (1965). In that work, he maintains that the classical liberal notion of tolerance has lost its radical character.

Once connected with the critique of religious prejudices and political authority, experimentation and the exercise of judgment, tolerance has turned into a bulwark for the status quo. Marcuse's argument once again relies on the idea that the medium is the message. Insofar as the culture industry presents all positions on any issue in a public forum, they all ultimately appear as having equal value. Tolerance as exhibited by the culture industry thus renders all truth claims relative—or, better, turns their acceptance into a matter of taste. Now it is not just beauty but *truth* that lies in the eye of the beholder. What happened to art has happened to the discourse. Both become subordinate to the commodity form whereby qualitative turns into merely quantitative differences. When considering imperialism and war, or assaults on the welfare state and creationism, one stance is as good as another. The mass media renders resistance no more legitimate than support.

Repressive tolerance is a real phenomenon. Fox News is a living embodiment of the concept. But that doesn't mitigate the problems associated with Marcuse's essay. There is, first of all, a difference between arguing that tolerance has lost is radical edge and that tolerance is repressive. The political emphasis is also misplaced. The real problem was never repressive tolerance but the *repression of tolerance*. Censorship is still rife and, historically, the Left has usually suffered the most when civil liberties were constricted in advanced industrial societies.

Marcuse's essay has little to say about criteria for judging what is to be censored, the bureaucracy required for instituting censorship, or the likelihood that such a bureaucracy will grow. It also ignores how the culture industry has often attacked intolerance and reactionary values: *All in the Family* and its main character, Archie Bunker, began a trend. Television sitcoms like *The Cosby Show* and *Good Times*, or *Will and Grace* and *Ellen*, may not have critically depicted the "real life" of oppressed and maligned groups. But they were progressive in the broader ethical and political agendas that they served. Talk about the integration of the gains that these subaltern groups have achieved, or how they strengthened the system, only begs the question: Were these gains domesticated or was the system itself forced to adapt and change?

Marcuse's *One-Dimensional Man* highlights the possibilities attendant upon redirecting technology to overcome scarcity and pacify existence. Advanced industrial society, however, still rests on a structural contradiction between the interests of the bourgeoisie (which buys labor power and controls the means of production) and the working class (which sells its labor power and stands in alienated relation to the means of production). But this objective contradiction is not subjectively perceived as such. Political consciousness on the part of the working class is lacking due to the real failings of communism, the seeming affluence of Western capitalism, and—perhaps above all—the culture industry.

Marcuse popularized that concept in the United States. Like other members of the Frankfurt School, indeed, he was deeply concerned with how it prefabricates experience and nullifies critical thinking. His perspective clearly builds upon *Dialectic of Enlightenment*. What should serve as the aesthetic sublimation of erotic and life-giving impulses into art is instead transformed by the culture industry as the work adapts itself to the logic of commerce. "Repressive de-sublimation" drains its liberating and critical potential. Individuals are thrown back on their own resources. Loneliness and alienation produce an ever greater reliance on the culture industry and participate in the happy consciousness. Popular art strengthens the system even as it diminishes the psychological capacity for exercising the utopian imagination. The popularity of an artwork produces its death throes.

But is it true that the popularity of a work necessarily invalidates its critical character or artistic radicalism? The seemingly endless array of rebels without a cause evince what Adorno called "non-conformist conformity" while the shallow cynicism and pseudo-heroic combat against imagined conspiracies offer what Paul Piccone—the mercurial editor of the journal *Telos* that brought critical theory to America—termed "artificial negativity."

But, surely, that is not the case with great artists like Charlie Chaplin or Bob Dylan or Francis Ford Coppola. Condemning the artistic quality of their works is possible only if they are denied the status of art by definition. Yet that is the claim made by Horkheimer, Adorno, and—albeit with a twist—even by Marcuse. It is the only position that fits the reification argument in *Dialectic of Enlightenment* and *One-Dimensional Man*.

Explanations are offered; qualifications are made; and strained justifications are introduced. At the end of the day, however, no popular artist was ever championed by the Frankfurt School. Most of its members simply didn't like popular culture. They had no feel for it, and they showed no interest in its achievements. Adorno stated in *Minima Moralia* that "every visit to the cinema leaves me, against all my vigilance, stupider and worse." He would later revise that statement. But the same sweeping judgment, the same overarching condemnation, occurs in his notorious essay "On Jazz" (1936). Adorno is never clear about what he means by "jazz." Whether it refers to the specific genre or popular music in general, however, is irrelevant. His essay offers no understanding of what is actually a tradition with its own canon. There is little discussion about the live experience of jazz, less about its connection with the blues, and still less about its origins or its evocation of lives dominated by racism and poverty. "On Jazz" is content to note the psychological regression and loss of individuality produced by supposedly illusory improvisation and simplistic syncopation by a mass phenomenon that is now (interestingly enough) even less popular than classical music.

"On Jazz" exhibits a profound cultural pessimism. It rests on general claims and it is unconcerned with distinguishing between artists or artistic works. Comparisons never emerge between say, Louis Armstrong and Paul Whiteman or Duke Ellington and his imitators. There is nothing about the great songs that were interpreted and reinterpreted by a host of extraordinary female vocalists.

To this extent, indeed, Adorno's essay reflects the undifferentiated image of a totally administered society that animated *Dialectic of Enlightenment*. The lyrics of songs sung by Bessie Smith, Ethel Waters, and Billie Holiday apparently don't inspire genuine resistance. What resistance should mean, however, remains as vague as ever. The same situation pertains to politics. Even Marcuse admitted as much when he wrote in *One-Dimensional Man*: "The critical theory of society possesses no concepts which could bridge the gap between the present and its future; holding no promise and showing no success, it remains negative. Thus, it wants to remain loyal to those who, without hope, have given and give their life to the Great Refusal."

Chapter 7
The great refusal

Critical theory was an important intellectual impetus for the European student movement of the 1960s. In the United States, however, most seminal works of critical theory were translated only during the 1970s. That was when journals like *Telos* and *New German Critique* began gaining an audience and publicizing its most important representatives. Complicated ideas about alienation, the domination of nature, regression, utopia, and the culture industry made critical theory relevant for young intellectuals who were coming of age amid the turbulence of the times and were trying to make sense of what was happening around them. But the rebellion and the solidarity of the young employed the culture industry. That made its radical character no less real. It soon enough became apparent that art is not a lost cause even after Auschwitz. The identification of culture with the happy consciousness is never quite as absolute—or not yet as absolute—as some might care to believe.

The new sensibility

Activists during the 1960s still understood critical theory within the context of Marxism. Herbert Marcuse insisted that transforming advanced industrial society required action by the working class. But he felt that its outlook had been manipulated by the culture industry, economic gains, and the political establishment. Revolutionary consciousness could arise only outside its ranks. Women, people of color, anti-imperialist movements at the periphery of the system, intellectuals, and bohemians might provide the working class not merely with a revolutionary spark, but with something more elusive: a new sensibility. These new catalysts of revolution would embody what Andre Breton originally termed the "great refusal."

Here, once again, critical theory evinces its connection with modernism, Breton was a legend among the European avant-garde and the guiding light of surrealism. He called for rebellion against the settled habits of everyday life and direct action by the proletariat against the state. Above all, however, Breton endorsed a form of art that rejected the familiar, the consensual, and the traditional. His aesthetic was dedicated to an assault upon narrative and linear rationality.

Both Benjamin and Adorno had been fascinated by surrealism during the 1930s. They, too, endorsed montage, stream of consciousness, the epiphany, and the liberation of the unconscious. Especially Benjamin saw surrealism as evoking a kind of "revolutionary intoxication" whose enemy was the everyday life of bourgeois society. The great refusal was understood by Marcuse as animating resistance to cruelty, exploitation, and the inhumane values of advanced industrial society.

An Essay on Liberation, among his most popular works, saw the great refusal as generating a utopian sensibility. That the young rebels embodied this is surely an exaggeration. The marginal groups were perhaps never quite that marginal. It is probably better to speak of burgeoning new social movements—partially generated by expanding labor markets—and strip them of revolutionary and utopian pretensions. Their most impressive successes were achieved through the courts and by political legislation. But it is easy to be too cynical. There was a widespread revulsion against war and the "military-industrial complex." There were radical demands for transparency and for democratic accountability. The "Great Society" programs of President Lyndon Johnson were responses to pressure from below by community-based organizations and new social movements. The "freedom riders" that fought for civil rights in the South were outsiders. In Europe and Latin America it was radical intellectuals like Rudi Dutschke and Danny Cohn-Bendit whose followers ignited the huge strike-wave of 1968 that was marked by a democratic ideal of *autogestion* that harked back to the workers' councils and the Paris Commune.

Environmentalism, animal rights, and an assault on male chauvinism were outgrowths of the new sensibility. Educational reform of a radical sort mixed with the demands of cultural modernists for the transformation of everyday life. Sexual mores and race relations changed. The quality of life emerged as a matter of fundamental concern—and, undoubtedly, aesthetic perceptions changed as well. The New Left evinced a deep appreciation of subjectivity. People of color, women, gays, and intellectuals sought to make sense of the world and gain a measure of existential meaning and purpose for themselves. The New Left was the first mass movement that privileged cultural transformation. That was what created its affinity for critical theory and the Frankfurt School.

Conservative attacks on the adversary culture in the 1980s in the United States, and then again in the aftermath of 9/11, brought with it an overarching attack on the welfare state and civil liberties in the name of nationalism, militarism, and imperialism. Marcuse anticipated something like this in *Counter-Revolution and Rev*olt (1972). He speculated about reactionary attempts to undermine the political interests and ideals associated with the new sensibility His own sensibility underwent not so much a change as a shift in emphasis. His last published work, *The Aesthetic Dimension* (1978), notes that its "debt to the aesthetic theory of

Theodor W. Adorno does not require any specific acknowledgment." There was still a hint of hope—but it was fading. The great refusal embodied in modernist art of an explicitly political sort (like that of Brecht) now exited the stage. Aesthetics should now affirm not the consciousness of a movement, or some new form of historical subject, but genuine individuality whose existence is imperiled by forces far grander than what the rebels of '68 imagined.

Utopia is always less a finished product than a longing for transcendence. Especially where the culture industry defines public life, where concepts are continually simplified and ideals are turned into platitudes, cultivation of that longing perhaps assumes value in its own right. That was certainly what Max Horkheimer came to believe toward the end of his life. He also knew that individual experience is easily manipulated and that the critical impulse within seeking transcendence cannot be taken for granted. There are drugs; there are preachers; there are cults; and always there are promises of redemption and bliss. The culture industry thrives on happiness. It is standardized and prepackaged. But real happiness contests a miserable reality. It speaks only to the experience of the particular individual—like the religious notion of grace.

In "The Ego and Freedom Movements" (1936), Horkheimer insisted that unconditional happiness cannot exist—only the longing for it. That longing denies all attempts by the commodity form and instrumental rationality to transform the qualitative into the quantitative and the sacred into the profane. Each of us has a natural desire for eternity, beauty, transcendence, salvation, and God—or what Horkheimer ultimately termed the "longing for the totally other." He makes no promises, depicts no ritual, and provides no church. But this longing provides the foundation for resisting the totally administered society and affirming individuality. The longing for the totally other has nothing in common with organized religion. Nevertheless, its reliance on negation incorporates its hopes for paradise and its ability to experientially affirm the self.

Ernst Bloch once said that the truth is a prayer. Yet the inexpressible is perhaps best expressed by music. It provides the encounter with what is deepest within us. In his classic *Philosophy of Modern Music* (1958), similarly, Adorno was obviously referring to redemption when he insisted that the intimation of "someone returning" is "expressive of all music, even in a world that deserves to die." There is a way in which all of this tends to identify negation and utopia with existential experience. Stripped of all determinations and mediations, intimations of clarity and hope can be elicited (though never defined) by religion, art, and philosophy. Hegel had viewed these domains of the mind as being rendered ever more distinct by historical progress. But that perspective is inverted by the Frankfurt School. Religion, art, and philosophy now become almost interchangeable in the inexpressible truth they project.

Whatever differences exist between them lack any practical significance. Freedom stands beyond mimesis–like God—and that is also true of hell. When Adorno noted that "there can be no poetry after Auschwitz," the oft-quoted and oft-revised line that concluded "Cultural Criticism and Society" (1951), it was meant in just this spirit. The religious injunction of Judaism now takes aesthetic form. The incarnation of evil, like the incarnation of good, can only be intimated and never depicted: no objectification of God can be perfect enough and no objectification of the Holocaust can be horrific enough. Adorno drew the radical implications of this position in *Minima Moralia* when he wrote: "only insofar as it withdraws from man can culture be faithful to man."

Embracing the negation

The Frankfurt School breathed the air of European modernism. From the last quarter of the nineteenth century until the Nazi triumph of 1933, it seemed, an international avant-garde was contesting an emerging mass society with its emphasis upon bureaucracy, standardization, scientific rationality, and the commodity form. Countless Impressionists, Cubists, Expressionists, Futurists, Dadaists, and Surrealists sought to experience the world anew. Through a blizzard of philosophical-aesthetic manifestos they launched an assault upon everything associated with the "realistic" purposes of art in the name of the utopian imagination and the liberation of individuality. Resistance shifted from the political to the cultural realm. Or, in the case of the Frankfurt School, the moment in which critical reflection provided by philosophy blends with the experiential intensity highlighted by aesthetics. The negation turned into the point of transcendental resistance in which subjectivity contests the ontology of false conditions.

The Frankfurt School was always suspicious of organized politics. Implicit in its views on alienation and reification was the belief that linking theory to practice would only further the plans of the terrible simplifiers. The dangers of anti-intellectualism seemed palpable, and in "Resignation" and the other essays comprising *Critical Models 2* (1969), Adorno expressed his contempt for those who say "enough talking already." The practice in which they wished to "join in" could never be radical enough given the way in which the culture industry would present it. Young people had lessons to learn from totalitarian movements with their propaganda apparatus and their contempt for the individual. Affirming individuality was the best response to the totally administered society. But there is something self-serving about all of this.

Activity that evidences a plausible connection between ends and means is not the same thing as action for its own sake or what Adorno termed "actionism." Theory is surely not reducible to practice. But this doesn't mean it should turn its back on illuminating the constraints and opportunities for change. That political activity does not always generate reflection is a hard lesson. Adorno was right to teach it. But his call to "think" sounds like the stern command of a provincial schoolteacher; it becomes a code word for standing above the fray. Resignation remains what it is: rejection of engagement and withdrawal from the organized project for institutional change.

Adorno's essay titled "Engagement," which is included in *Notes on Literature* (1969), is a direct assault on Bertolt Brecht and Jean-Paul Sartre. Both of them were sympathetic to communism and both emphasized the need to connect literature with a partisan view of political trends. Sartre wrote in *What Is Literature?* (1947) that no great novel can be written that endorses anti-Semitism. With an eye cast on Brecht's didactic plays like *The Measures Taken* (1930), which contains the famous line "the party has a thousand eyes, we have only two," Adorno retorted that no great novel can be written in praise of the Moscow trials either. He always believed that the idea of a politically engaged literature is a contradiction in terms. It can offer neither critique of the totality (since the artwork is always partisan in its politics) nor any meaningful utopian vision (since genuine happiness always stands beyond objectification).

The ability to depict the eradication of subjectivity in a totally administered society, a nightmarish world of bureaucracy with no exit and no meaning, is precisely what made Franz Kafka's writings so seminal for this brand of critical theory. Something is always elusive in Kafka. What? Not only subjectivity, whether of the character or the onlooker, but the manner in which it is elicited.

Aesthetic Theory (1969) projects notions of subjectivity, freedom, and utopia that resist all objectification. Adorno's towering work—that demonstrates his extraordinary intellectual power and justifies his enduring appeal—stresses the tensions arising within the artwork as a social monad. Kant's view of aesthetic experience as exhibiting a kind of purposeful purposelessness thus exists within the same phenomenon that, following Marx, embodies specific forms of repression. Conflicts are embedded in the work between form and content, reflection and experience, technique and inspiration, utopian hope and anthropological negation. The work of art is thus a "force field" of conflicting tensions. Critical aesthetics should highlight them. Its true aim is not to create a shared understanding of the world through some common identification with characters, narratives, and themes but, instead, to intensify experience. That is why, according to Adorno, the paradigmatic moment of art is "fireworks."

Not many artists are capable of generating this moment, and Adorno's essay on a play by Samuel Beckett, *Understanding Endgame* (1961), is both a masterful investigation of dramatic technique and a superb condensation of his general aesthetic outlook. Beckett creates a world of illusion that each experiences differently. Its "truth content" appears in its aesthetically formed resistance to the world of reification and alienation. The character of its response, however, is inexpressible: it is rendered unique for each member of the audience.

The longing for the totally other implicitly makes itself felt. Adorno was surely aware of that. From Benjamin, after all, he had learned that aesthetic critique rests on the (hopeless) hope of redemption. There are no good old days as romantics and conservatives still tend to think. Beckett's *Happy Days* (1961) offers a searing indictment of that idea with its characters ultimately buried in sand up to the neck while indulging in recollections of the past that never occurred. Both of these plays by Beckett are minimalist in their staging and dialogue. It should be noted that Adorno always sought to prevent the use of aesthetic form from degenerating into formalism and utopian longing from collapsing into irrationalism. His corrective lies in the critical connection of the work to the ontology of false conditions and its rejection of all facile attempts to live the wrong life rightly.

Negative Dialectics (1966) is the philosophical articulation of this enterprise. Its starting point is a metacritique of idealism that builds upon *Three Studies on Hegel* (1963). The break between history and freedom once again becomes the centerpiece of the argument. No prefabricated harmony is possible between the individual and society. Creating an identity between subject and object is self-defeating. History is the realm of un-freedom, the increasing subjugation of subjectivity, and the triumph of necessity and instrumental rationality over happiness and subjectivity. Belief in the march of progress has been invalidated by the triumph of totalitarianism. Conceptualizing the individual in universal terms was a mistake from the beginning.

Kant succumbed to that idea. So did Hegel and Marx. Their teleological outlook seemed to justify every sacrifice in the name

8. According to the interpretation by T. W. Adorno, *Endgame* by Samuel Beckett elicits subjectivity and thereby serves to resist the totally administered society. This photograph shows a scene from the play.

of bringing about an ill-fated unity between subject and object. Subjugated either to the World Spirit or the working class, the individual was left without experiential moorings and, effectively, disempowered,

Negative Dialectics and the *Three Studies on Hegel* contest this set of assumptions. Each shows how the Hegelian "negation of the negation" that supposedly produces ever more positive determinations of freedom actually undermines autonomy through increasing reification. These works by Adorno validate the negation in its own right without reference to any historical understanding of progress. Resolution of the tensions between the individual and society is impossible. The attempt to project it is a self-defeating enterprise. Negative dialectics affirms instead the non-identity between subject and object, the individual and society, as well as the particular and the universal. Non-identity, however, cannot simply be proclaimed. Critical reflection is required to explain how it is expressed in any particular circumstance and how the given experience escapes objectification.

Adorno puts the matter clearly in one of his 1965 lectures that dealt with *Negative Dialectics*: "[P]hilosophy is the contradictory effort to say, through mediation and contextualization, what cannot be said." The longing for the totally other fosters a situation in which the conceptual must constantly seek to grasp the non-conceptual. The connection is palpable between Adorno's outlook and that of Beckett in *The Unnamable* (1953): "I can't go on. I will go on."

Resistance involves rejecting the ontology of false conditions without thinking it can be changed. The philosophical blends with the aesthetic and the religious as well. Hegel is turned not on his head, but inside out: the qualitative distinctions between the three moments of his Absolute Idea are abolished. There remains only reflection upon the indefinable and indeterminate longing for freedom that has been elicited by the reality that denies its realization. Herein is the last vestige of solidarity. The metacritique has no room for institutions or organizations capable of concretely fostering (or inhibiting) solidarity in a world dominated by the commodity form, bureaucratic hierarchy, and the culture industry.

Solidarity, like resistance, thus takes a new metaphysical form. The logic of historical materialism immanently insists upon such a change. Communism is dead, social democracy has been domesticated, and the culture industry has rendered it impossible to conceive of a transformative agent. Reality itself calls for privileging metaphysics over materialism. In *Negative Dialectics*, therefore, Adorno could write that "philosophy, which once seemed obsolete, lives on because the moment to realize it was missed."

Chapter 8
From resignation to renewal

Critical theory was originally intended as an alternative to mainstream forms of both metaphysics and materialism. Its aim was to illuminate hidden sources of repression and neglected transformative possibilities. Following the outbreak of World War II, however, the Frankfurt School concluded that liberating alternatives had vanished. Critical theory awoke in Hegel's night where all cows are black. Resistance took an increasingly existential form. It now rested on intensifying the non-identity between the individual and society. The "system" became the point of reference. Negation confronted the ontology of false conditions. Hints of utopia contested civilization. "He wants all or nothing," Brecht once wrote, "and in response to this challenge the world usually answers: then better nothing."

A critical theory of society

The Frankfurt School first achieved popularity in the United States by appealing to what Martin Jay, its first historian, termed "the generation of 1968." Well into the 1980s, critical theory was still considered eccentric in mainstream academic circles and somewhat exotic even among progressive intellectuals. With the collapse of the New Left, however, the Frankfurt School became institutionalized within the academy. Critical legal studies, critical race theory, critical gender studies began interrogating prevailing paradigms and assumptions. As subaltern groups emerged from the shadows of public life, however, the integrated assault upon an integrated system of domination began to erode. New emphasis was placed on contesting master narratives, the established canons of the Western tradition, and even popular culture entered the mix. The critical theory of society, its coherence, was becoming imperiled. Its transformative purpose was taking increasingly arbitrary forms.

New proposals have not been forthcoming for dealing with imperialist exploits, economic contradictions, the state, mass media, and the character of resistance in modern society. The negation is casting a pall over critical theory. The intellectual heir of Hegel and Marx now lacks an understanding of power and, as a consequence, the ability to confront the imbalance of power. Correctives exist in some of the more neglected writings of the Frankfurt School.

Essays like "State Capitalism" (1941) by Friedrich Pollock provide a starting point. Its analysis of the "command economy" forces us to consider whether talk of the free market is anachronistic and whether old notions of nationalization are equivalent with socialism. "Confining Conditions and Revolutionary Breakthroughs" (1965) by Otto Kirchheimer warns of tendencies of the modern state to render emergency powers "normal." Posthumously published essays like "A History of the Doctrine of Social Change" and "Theories of Social Change" by Herbert Marcuse and Franz Neumann speak to the presuppositions that a genuinely critical theory of society must confront

Contemporary philosophical and literary offshoots of critical theory usually treat power as an artificial social or linguistic construct. The accumulation process disappears, the system takes on a life of its own, and individuals are left to find a common basis for solidarity in notions of recognition or care that lack any institutional or organizational referent. Domination is thereby severed from exploitation and principle is divorced from interest. An alternative to the overtly metaphysical and subjective trends within critical theory is offered by Jürgen Habermas.

Communication is seen by him as inherently grounded in the open character of the discourse, the recognition of each participant as equal, and the willingness of each to change his mind when faced with a better argument, Communication, in short, does not require some kind of metaphysical ethic separate from practice. It harbors its own "universal pragmatics." Or, to put it another way, communicative ethics preserves autonomy while fostering solidarity in the very desire to communicate. Those who deny the norms of this ethic, or who exercise power arbitrarily, deny the very means they use to persuade: they find themselves caught, philosophically speaking, in a "performative contradiction."

But the metaphysical turn in critical theory has resisted—or, better, incorporated—Habermas' challenge. *Robert's Rules of Order* embodies similar principles. Whether this handbook for guiding public meetings is taken seriously by the participants, of course, is another matter. The practical contribution of the universal pragmatics is not self-evident. Communicative ethics allows liberals and rationalists to congratulate themselves whenever they avoid falling into a performative contradiction. Many of their political adversaries, however, privilege intuition and experience in evaluating truth claims, Others who are more extreme have no interest at all in truth claims. Most of these people would probably respond, when caught in a performative contradiction, so what?

Speaking truth to power presupposes the ability to render it visible—and concrete. *The Authoritarian Personality* (1950) renders an important service in this regard. Edited by Adorno, and various other collaborators, it notes psychological differences between individuals and calls for re-educating not merely the anti-Semite in particular but the parochial and bigoted personality in general. Using empirical techniques like the famous "f-scale" or "fascism scale," its authors illuminate the reactionary character structure and castigate its effects. They emphasize how the authoritarian personality shows contempt for the outsider, the new, and the different. They highlight its penchant for violence, and they plead for policies fostering tolerance.

On first blush, of course, there is something strange about this coming from the inventor of negative dialectics. The study smacks of mass education and adaptation to establishmentarian standards. Potential now seemingly exists for intervening in what elsewhere is considered a seamless whole. But, then, there is the warning that the authoritarian and non-authoritarian personalities are different less in kind than in degree. The qualitative distinction between them appears more illusory than real. The authors vacillate between embracing reform and denying its utility.

In his *Introduction to Sociology* (2000), and other works, Adorno stated his opposition to civic passivity and his support for progressive reform. But the question of agency was left hanging in the abstract. He also never dealt with the impact of reform on the totally administered society or the ontology of false conditions. That Adorno should have undertaken a critique of the exchange relationship under capitalism does not change matters. The totally administered society and the genuine negativity it requires are both insulated from any commonly accepted notion of political action. In "Theory, Practice, and Moral Philosophy (2001)," therefore, Adorno can envision a new form of practice that "resists the call of practicality" and that, precisely because it rejects any instrumental usage, thereby "contains a practical element within itself." Or, more simply, theory becomes practice—though it need contribute nothing with concrete implications for liberating society.

9. A new direction for critical theory finds its source in the famous inscription on the statue marking Karl Marx's grave site in London: "Philosophers have only interpreted the world. The point is to change it!"

Scrutiny is required of the metaphysical turn taken by critical theory along with categories like the totally administered society and the ontology of false conditions. The empirical claims of the Frankfurt School concerning the former are invalid and the philosophical reliance on the latter doesn't help make them valid. Eliminating the proletariat as a revolutionary agent did not result in a totally administered society but rather in splits among the elite—or the ruling class—over particular social policies, cultural values, and institutional developments. These have very different effects upon working people and subaltern groups. Opposition still exists between what Marx called the political economy of capital and the political economy of labor.

Neglecting real ideological and material conflicts of interest in the name of an image like the totally administered society hinders the ability to interpret events in meaningful and innovative ways. More is involved than communicative misunderstanding or the imperiled life-world. Meaningful notions of solidarity refer to actual conflicts within society. Without privileging them, indeed, both resistance and domination lose their historical specificity and, hence, their concreteness. They become just another pair of words.

Alienation and reification once spoke to the experience of domination and the imperative of transformative practice. Now they mostly serve to excuse inaction. In order to make these concepts salient once again, in my opinion, it is important to distinguish between them. It is probably best to begin in the following way: Alienation was defined by the young Marx with an eye on overcoming the division of labor and reasserting human control over the production process.

In the twentieth century, however, alienation has taken on other connotations. Elusive and unyielding, it has become associated with feelings of guilt, fear, mortality, and meaninglessness. Utopia is the only response to alienation or, better, the existential problems that plague us and the anthropological foundations of our existence. Reification should, by contrast, be considered fungible—and the target for social action. It exhibits less the framework for advanced industrial society than the impact of its workings. Instrumental rationality is nothing more than a mathematical technique for dealing efficiently with scarcity. It can empower victims of pre-capitalist prejudices as easily as it can reduce the worker to a cost of production and human beings to disposable resources.

What counts is not the formal character of bureaucracy and instrumental rationality but rather the (often hidden) values and interests informing how they are employed. Critical theory should be scrutinizing the purposive ends or, better, the different priorities and interests embedded in the policies and institutions that are shaping our lives. Obsession with the formal character of instrumental rationality is itself an expression of reification that has had debilitating effects on the interpretation of science and its methods.

Critical theory originally confronted orthodox Marxism by severing the inquiry into society from the inquiry into nature. Treating instrumental rationality in terms of epistemological formalism, however, undermines that distinction. Sociological attempts to contextualize scientific theories and technological innovations are both legitimate and salient. It is another matter, however, for a normative theory to judge the internal workings of scientific theories and techniques. To put it crudely, critical theory can offer fruitful perspectives on the historical genesis and social uses of, say, the theory of relativity introduced by Albert Einstein. But it should not attempt to make philosophical judgments about its truth character.

Contesting reification does not obliterate the need for disciplinary expertise and the ability to know what one is talking about. Utopian visions of a new science, especially one that lacks criteria for verifying its truth claims, are also defined by the reification they oppose. Critical theory would be better served by building upon the notion of "falsifiability" that Sir Karl Popper introduced in *The Logic of Scientific Discovery* (1959). The spirited "positivism debate" of the 1960s between the Frankfurt School and its more scientifically inclined rivals treat this matter and others from a number of fascinating perspectives. Advocates of critical theory, however, usually tend to underestimate the methodological importance and practical implications of viewing scientific truth claims as provisional and open to revision in light of future research. Such a stance, indeed, fits neatly into the critical enterprise.

To be sure: scientific paradigms and their criteria for verifying truth claims will change down the line. Even "paradigm shifts" will take place. Thomas Kuhn suggested in his classic *The Structure of Scientific Revolutions* (1962), however, that they will occur because new problems are encountered that the old scientific methods cannot adequately address—not because philosophers engage in some abstract indictment of science based on an inarticulate utopian vision.

Articulate utopian approaches, by contrast, might have something to offer. Without jettisoning the natural sciences, but while circumscribing their conceptual applicability, Ernst Bloch's *Avicenna and the Aristotelian Left* (1949) offers an innovative cosmological view of nature predicated on a reinterpretation of Aristotle. Highlighting his neglected notions of potentiality and dynamism for understanding the life world, employing Avicenna and Averroes to juxtapose the living quality of nature (*natura naturans*) against its empirical expressions (*natura naturata*), this work generated a view of the ecosystem that would have profound significance for modern ecology and environmentalism.

Nature is seen by Bloch as irreducible to its empirical constituents, (which is precisely what capitalist rationality assumes), and as a life-sustaining element of humanity. Scientific rationality of the traditional sort has its place, but the cosmological element within nature sets boundaries for what instrumental rationality can ascertain and projects ethical priorities for its employment. The ecosystem becomes the target of cultivation and preservation. Recognizing the subject or life-sustaining quality of nature, which is hidden behind its objective manifestations, is the precondition for genuine radicalism and any meaningful notion of utopia. Whatever its problems, therefore, Bloch's speculative inquiry into materialism has social implications: its critique presents a positive conceptual response to existing environmental assumptions that have had such devastating implications.

Engaging in critique need not require an anthropological break with reality. Norms are required in order to evaluate the alternatives on any given issue. But they hang in the abstract unless related to often conflicting interests and the ability to realize them. Power is an ineradicable element of modern society. It is neither an artificial construct nor an arbitrary determination of the will. Its mediations and determinations define the character of society and the political reaction to it. Freedom becomes, once again, the insight into necessity.

Franz Neumann alludes to these matters in his classic essays, "Approaches to the Study of Power (1950) and "The Concept of Freedom." He notes that the issue for modern society is much less the curtailment of political power than its reasonable employment. Only by drawing this distinction is it possible to prevent the theory of reification from itself becoming reified. Critique begins with its commitment to freedom. For this to become concrete, however, theory needs to engage the matter of power. Just as institutions can retain too much power so is it possible for them to retain too little. Competing institutional visions will offer qualitatively different policy options. Criteria are necessary for distinguishing between rational and irrational forms of authority and policy. A genuinely critical theory of society should provide them.

The politics of enlightenment

Enlightenment theory and practice focused upon curtailing the arbitrary exercise of institutional power, fostering pluralism, and enabling the exercise of individuality. Not the "Great Refusal" but this complex of ethical and political themes informed the great progressive movements of the past. That was the case with the socialist labor movement, the civil rights movement, the women's liberation movement, the anti-communist uprisings in Eastern Europe, and the most democratic and egalitarian trends within world religions and the once colonized world. The implication is clear: invigorating the transformative purpose of critical theory calls for revising its primarily negative view of the enlightenment legacy.

Walter Benjamin's *German People* (1933) perhaps provides a place to begin. It is composed of letters that he collected over the years. They were written not by famous people but rather by their friends, relatives, or associates. These were everyday people inspired by enlightenment ideals like Kant's brother or Goethe's close friend. This little book rebukes the common wisdom. The Enlightenment extended beyond a small circle of intellectuals. Its political values and cultural concerns spoke to those who sought a more decent and liberal world.

The Frankfurt School was profoundly mistaken in thinking that the Enlightenment—or, better, its scientific rationality—should be interpreted as triumphant or in isolation from the theory and practice of its rivals. Enlightenment thinking has always been on the defensive. That remains the case. From the "Know-Nothings" of the early nineteenth century to the Ku Klux Klan to the "America Firsters" to the "Tea-Baggers" of our own time, indeed, the United States has suffered from what Richard Hofstadter called a "paranoid" strain in its politics. The most cursory look at world events further justifies this assessment. Human rights, tolerance, cosmopolitan ideals, (and even science) are most everywhere under siege—or, at least, contested—by forces of religious fanaticism, cultural provincialism, and authoritarian reaction.

Ernst Bloch's *Heritage of Our Times* (1935) argues that modernity generates resentment and support for atavistic values by premodern constituencies that feel themselves imperiled by its effects. In analyzing fascism, he investigates contradictions existing in a variety of social spheres that have been carried over from one period to the next in which they assume a new character. If capitalist society is shaped by specific conflicts of class interest, for example, it also exhibits pre-capitalist (and thus nonsynchronous) problems with sexism or racism or even leadership that require previously unanticipated solutions. If only for this reason the future is always open. That the political and ideological opponents of modernity can still achieve power is what this perspective has to teach.

In castigating the Enlightenment, the Frankfurt School ignored what Sir Isaiah Berlin first termed the Counter-Enlightenment. Luminaries of the reaction like Johann Georg Hamann were of an inferior intellectual caliber than their liberal opponents. They reveal themselves as so authoritarian, narrow-minded, and bigoted that they are barely worth reading today. In forgetting about them, however, criticisms of the Enlightenment offered by the Frankfurt School ultimately prove distorted. The phenomenon is judged out of context and with an abstract point of reference.

Liberal republicanism and democratic socialism both have their roots in the Enlightenment. Its partisans were in the forefront of those contesting the exercise of arbitrary power by unaccountable institutions. But they also contributed to the transformation of civil society through their attack on elementary forms of cruelty, religious dogmatism, illiteracy, superstition, xenophobia, and impolite behavior. The enlightenment legacy has only gained in its social and political relevance. There are three basic political points for critical theory to consider:

1) Enlightenment ideals evince an elective affinity with anti-authoritarian movements. Left wing movements tend to privilege cosmopolitanism over parochialism, reason over intuition, skepticism over tradition, and liberty over authority. It only makes sense that right-wing movements should embrace the Counter-Enlightenment. Two movements were in conflict from the start. The dialectic of enlightenment is a fiction.

2) Enlightenment norms have an inherently critical character. Victims of prejudice inevitably refer to them when calling for remedial action. No custom or tradition, moreover, is exempt from scrutiny. Universal norms associated with the Enlightenment contest the personal prejudices held even by many of its most notable representatives.

3) Enlightenment principles foster pluralism. They expressly reject integral nationalism and the organic community. They also highlight tolerance, experimentation, and autonomy. Only insofar as the liberal rule of law is operative is it possible to speak about the free and practical exercise of subjectivity.

None of this was fully appreciated by the inner circle of the Frankfurt School—and the implications are apparent in its treatment of mass education and the culture industry. Insofar as works of art are treated no differently than other commodities, the culture industry is seen by the Frankfurt School as standardizing aesthetic experience and imperiling subjectivity. An inevitable loss of intellectual standards takes place through its obsession with maximizing profits by constantly lowering the lowest common denominator. Popularity integrates the work into the system. Its critical character and its ability to project an emancipated alternative therefore necessarily diminish. Only highly complex and sophisticated artworks can subsequently elicit those repressed utopian images and experiences of subjectivity that are capable of resisting the debilitating impulses of mass society.

However, there is nothing stagnant about the culture industry. Its aesthetic and technological inventions have been astonishing. It has fostered pluralism by generating multiple publics—each with its own standards of judgment and purpose. Many of its works challenge the status quo and reification. But that is not really the point. Insisting that genuine art must somehow contest the ontology of false conditions is nostalgia for the seminar room masquerading as radicalism.

Critical theory thereby lays itself open to caricature: its negation appears as the liberator incapable of either identifying the form that liberation should take or dealing with the embrace of oppression by the oppressed. Especially the adherents of negative dialectics never seem willing to put anything on the table other than their completely arbitrary taste for what constitutes resistance. Culture has always been used to maintain the rule of the powerful and the submission of the powerless. The ruling ideas," wrote Brecht in *Saint Joan of the Stockyards* (1929), "are the ideas of those who rule." With its abstract preoccupations, however, the Frankfurt School strips resistance to those ideas of any material referent.

Ideological conflicts within the cultural apparatus remain unspecified and indeterminate. Extreme populist tendencies on the Left may condemn complexity, ignore the canon, and dismiss the idea of classic works in ways that render it complicit in its own oppression. Yet critical theory might benefit from a bit less emphasis on the way in which the culture industry manipulates art than with its still untapped potential for shaping progressive political awareness.

Saturday Night Live and the comedienne Tina Fey helped demolish Governor Sarah Palin—the notorious vice-presidential choice of Senator John McCain and the Republicans in 2008—at least for that campaign. Mass media has, of course, been employed by right wing demagogues. But the culture industry is best conceived as what the critical philosopher Douglas Kellner termed a "contested terrain" in which battles are constantly taking place between unequal combatants with opposed ideological visions and values. Or, to put it another way, the culture industry is a branch of commodity production that *can* prove critical of commodity production.

Walter Benjamin treated such themes in "The Work of Art in the Age of Its Technological Reproducibility" (1935). This famous essay juxtaposes the premodern against the modern experience of painting. Taking place in a religious context, the premodern encounter with a painting is bathed in an "aura": the onlooker finds the work unique, authentic, a living symbol beyond the techniques used to produce it, and grounded within a palpable tradition. The technological ability to reproduce the work—think of a painting by Picasso turned into a poster adorning the wall of a college student—strips away its aura, its uniqueness, its authenticity, and its grounding in a fixed tradition. The loss of aura can intensify feelings of alienation and the appeal of reactionary movements intent upon providing an illusory sense of belonging. But the erosion of aura can also open the work to critical reflection or what Benjamin termed "a heightened presence of mind."

Two possibilities subsequently present themselves: either the audience succumbs to emotional manipulation in an inauthentic attempt to experience what can no longer be experienced or it employs critical reflection to foster existential and political awareness. Too often, however, critics of the culture industry essentially deny that choice: the loss of aura is usually understood as presaging the manipulation of subjectivity and justifying the estrangement of art from the tastes and interests of the broader public.

Entertainment and reflection are not always mutually exclusive. Alternative media and cyberspace offer new options for progressive forces. Technical virtuosity also need not prove self-indulgent. Karl Krauss, who was much revered by Adorno, attacked the press and the conformist intellectuals of his time with satirical venom and a linguistic facility rarely found today. But Kraus's assault on the "failure of the imagination" that marked his time had a concrete focus: it was directed at cultural luminaries who were unable to envision the practical implications of their words.

Similar concerns mark an experimental—if highly controversial— novel like *Human Smoke* (2008) by Nicholson Baker. That work about the interwar period and the genesis of genocide employs hundreds of citations and anecdotes for the reader to organize in a constellation that analyzes the terrible dynamics of political violence, disparages mythical icons, reclaims forgotten men and women of conscience, and crystallizes the dignity of pacifism. It is possible to disagree with the author's conclusions, but impossible to ignore the critical perspective on history that he brings to bear or the ethical impulses informing his work. Enough popular intellectuals inside and outside the culture industry are engaged in producing new constellations and rubbing history against the grain—often with a political purpose.

The transformative impulse

Critical theory was originally intended as an interdisciplinary enterprise to which each might bring his or her unique disciplinary talent and expertise. Its representatives highlighted the relation between philosophy and politics, society and psychology, culture and liberation. They conceived of the totality and changed the way in which the social sciences, the humanities, and even interpreters of the natural sciences look at the world.

The Frankfurt School called outworn concepts into question. They looked at cultural ruins and lost hopes and what hegemonic cultural forces had ignored or repressed. They demanded that those committed to the ideals of liberation respond to new contingencies and new constraints. They also intimated the need for a new understanding of the relation between theory and practice. It is a proud legacy that is worth preserving—although without slavish devotion to this or that position or prophecy. Critical theory has new conditions to confront: the world has grown larger, new encounters with old civilizations have taken place, identities have multiplied, and—perhaps for the first time—it is possible to speak about a global economy and cultural system.

When Max Horkheimer took over the Institute, he hoped that critical theory would become a kind of public philosophy rather than yet another academic specialty that catered to an audience of experts. If this is still the goal, then critical theorists need to stop using the style of a tax form and abandon a one-sided analysis of mass culture based on the proposition that popularity—or clarity—is somehow inherently detrimental to the radicalism of a work.

Fostering a radical public philosophy is possible only by interrogating public problems and offering alternatives to the ways in which society stunts individuality. Critical theory has too long indulged what Thomas Mann first called a "power-protected inwardness." New aims and methods are necessary to illuminate imbalances of social, economic, and political power with an eye on the prospects for intervention.

Such an enterprise rests on clarifying the values and interests that existing ideologies and institutions tend to hide—so that everyday people can judge them and respond appropriately. C. Wright Mills made just this point in *The Sociological Imagination* (1960). In that classic work, which was strongly influenced by critical theory, this noted radical thinker called upon academics and intellectuals to transform "private troubles into public issues." Women have already turned incest and spousal abuse from private into public concerns; gay and lesbian citizens have advocated the need for legislation against "hate crimes"; people of color are challenging institutional racism; and countless other attempts have been made—and are still being made—to render the myriad institutions of the powerful accountable to the disempowered.

Agency has not disappeared from the world. Radical social movements still exist. But they are divided by deep and abiding differences. There is competition for resources, loyalty, and publicity. Incentives exist for organized interest groups to engage in the moral economy of the separate deal—so that the whole of the Left becomes less than the sum of its parts. Critical theory can help in coordinating interests with new categories and new principles. It has other tasks as well.

Democracy remains unfinished; cosmopolitanism is challenged by identity; socialism requires a new definition; and class ideals still await realization. The cultural inheritance of the past has still not been reclaimed; our experience of the world is still too narrow; and the ability of audiences to learn still requires criteria concerning what needs to be taught. New forms of redemption may still exist for the neglected utopian shards that have been littered throughout history. Engaging these matters requires an interdisciplinary outlook informed by liberating norms. There is always room for the discussion of regulative ideals like justice, liberty, and the like.

That is also the case for ontological categories dealing with the structure and meaning of existence. But there are better things for critical theorists to do than indulge what has become an obsession with attempting to express the inexpressible. Better to identify what is apparent but unrecognized, painful yet remediable, and repressed yet empowering. Only by confronting the world with a multifaceted transformative project can critical theory reassert its uniqueness and the salience of its animating ideals: solidarity, resistance, and freedom.

Further reading

Chapter 1

Illuminations: The Critical Theory Web Site. www.uta.edu/huma/illuminations/

Arato, Andrew, and Eike Gebhardt, eds. *The Essential Frankfurt School Reader*. New York: Continuum, 1982.

Benhabib, Seyla, et al., eds. *On Max Horkheimer* Cambridge, MA: MIT Press, 1995.

Bronner, Stephen Eric. *Of Critical Theory and Its Theorists*. 2nd ed. New York: Routledge, 2002.

Bronner, Stephen Eric, and Douglas Kellner, eds. *Critical Theory and Society*. New York: Routledge, 1989.

Habermas, Jürgen. *Philosophical-Political Profiles*. Translated by Frederick Lawrence. Cambridge, MA: MIT Press, 1983.

Jay, Martin. *The Dialectical Imagination*. Berkeley: University of California Press, 1996.

Lowenthal, Leo. *Critical Theory and Frankfurt Theorists: Lectures-Correspondence-Conversations*. New Brunswick, NJ: Transaction, 1989.

Tar, Zoltan. *The Frankfurt School*. New York: Schocken, 1985.

Wheatland, Thomas P. *The Frankfurt School in America: A Transatlantic Odyssey*. Minneapolis: University of Minnesota Press, 2009.

Wiggershaus, Rolf. *The Frankfurt School: Its History, Theories, and Political Significance*. Translated by Michael Robertson. Cambridge: Polity Press, 1994.

Chapter 2

Arato, Andrew, and Paul Breines. *The Young Lukacs and the Origins of Western Marxism*. New York: Seabury, 1979.

Dubiel, Helmut. *Theory and Politics: Studies in the Development of Critical Theory*. Translated by Benjamin Gregg. Cambridge, MA: MIT Press, 1985.

Forgasc, David, ed. *The Antonio Gramsci Reader 1916–1935*. New York: New York University Press, 2000.

Honneth, Axel. *Disrespect: The Normative Foundations of Critical Theory*. Cambridge: Polity Press, 2007.

Horkheimer, Max. *Critical Theory*. Translated by Matthew J. O'Connell. New York: Seabury Press, 1973.

———. *A Life in Letters: Selected Correspondence*. Edited and translated by Manfred R. Jacobson and Evelyn M. Jacobson. Lincoln: University of Nebraska Press, 2007.

Jay, Martin. *Marxism and the Totality: Adventures of a Concept from Lukacs to Habermas*. Berkeley: University of California Press, 1996.

Jones, Steven J. *Antonio Gramsci*. New York: Routledge, 2006.

Kellner, Douglas. *Critical Theory, Marxism, and Modernity*. Baltimore: Johns Hopkins University Press, 1989.

Korsch, Karl. *Revolutionary Theory*. Edited by Douglas Kellner. Austin: University of Texas Press, 1974.

Merleau-Ponty, Maurice. *Adventures of the Dialectic*. Translated by Joseph Bien. Evanston, IL: Northwestern University Press, 1973.

Morton, Adam. *Unraveling Gramsci: Hegemony and Passive Revolution in the Global Economy*. London: Pluto Press, 2007.

Rush, Fred, ed. *Cambridge Companion to Critical Theory*. New York: Cambridge University Press, 2004.

Chapter 3

Benjamin, Walter. *Illuminations*. Edited by Hannah Arendt. Translated by Harry Zohn. New York: Schocken, 1969.

Berman, Marshall. *Adventures in Marxism*. London: Verso, 1999.

Easton, Loyd D., and Kurt H. Guddat, eds. and trans. New York: Doubleday, 1967.

Feenberg, Andrew. *Alternative Modernity: The Technical Turn in Philosophy and Social Theory*. Berkeley: University of California Press: 1995.

Gerth, H. H., and C. Wright Mills, eds. *From Max Weber: Essays in Sociology*. New York: Oxford University Press, 1958.

Honneth, Axel. *Reification: A New Look at an Old Idea with Judith Butler, Raymond Geuss, and Jonathan Leader*. Edited by Martin Jay. New York: Oxford University Press, 2008.

Marcuse, Herbert. *From Luther to Popper: Studies in Critical Philosophy*. Boston: Beacon Press, 1991.

Ollman, Bertell. *Alienation: Marx's Concept of Man in Capitalist Society*. New York: Oxford University Press, 1977.

Schmitt, Richard. *Alienation and Freedom*. Boulder: Westview Press, 2002.

Chapter 4

Adorno, Theodor W., et al. *The Positivist Dispute in German Sociology*. Translated by Glyn Adey and David Frisby. London: Heinemann, 1976.

Bobbio, Norberto. *Ideological Profile of Twentieth Century Italy*. Translated by Lydia G. Cochrane. Princeton, NJ: Princeton University Press, 1995.

Bronner, Stephen Eric. *Reclaiming the Enlightenment: Toward a Politics of Radical Engagement*. New York: Columbia University Press, 2004.

———. *A Rumor About the Jews: Anti-Semitism, Conspiracy, and the Protocols of Zion*. New York: Oxford University Press, 2004.

Marcuse, Herbert. *Negations: Essays in Critical Theory*. Beacon Press: Boston, 1969.

Rabinbach, Anson. *In the Shadow of Catastrophe: German Intellectuals Between Apocalypse and Enlightenment*. Berkeley: University of California Press, 2001.

Chapter 5

Abromeit, John, and W. Mark Cobb, eds. *Herbert Marcuse: A Critical Reader*. New York: Routledge, 2003.

Buck-Morss, Susan. *Dialectics of Seeing: Walter Benjamin and the Arcades Project*. Cambridge, MA: MIT Press, 1991.

Daniel, James Owen, and Tom Moylan, eds. *Not Yet: Reconsidering Ernst Bloch*. London: Verso, 1997.

Feenberg, Andrew, ed. *Essential Marcuse*. Boston: Beacon Press, 2007.

Habermas, Jürgen. *Toward A Rational Society: Student Protest, Science, and Politics*. Boston: Beacon Press, 1970.

Kellner, Douglas, et al. *On Marcuse*. Boston: Sense Publishers, 2008.

Taylor, Ronald, ed. *Aesthetics and Politics: The Key Texts to the Classic Debates in German Marxism*. New York: Verso, 2007.

Wolin, Richard. *Walter Benjamin: An Aesthetic of Redemption*. New York: Columbia University Press, 1982.

Chapter 6

Adorno, Theodor W. *The Culture Industry: Selected Essays on Mass Culture*. Edited by J. M. Bernstein. New York: Routledge, 2001.

———. *Prisms*. Translated by Samuel Weber and Shierry Weber. Cambridge, MA: MIT Press, 1994.

———. *The Stars Down to Earth and Other Essays on the Irrational in Culture*. Edited by Stephen Crook. New York: Routledge, 1994.

Kellner, Douglas. *Media Spectacle and the Crisis of Democracy: Terrorism, War, and Election Battles*. Denver: Paradigm, 2005.

Negt, Oskar, and Alexander Kluge. *Public Sphere and Experience: Toward an Analysis of the Bourgeois and Proletarian Public Sphere*. Translated by Peter Labanyi. Minneapolis: University of Minnesota Press, 1993.

Ritzer, George. *The McDonaldization Thesis: Explorations and Extensions*. London: Sage, 1998.

Scholem, Gershom. *Walter Benjamin: The Story of a Friendship*. Translated by Harry Zohn. New York: Schocken, 1981.

Wolff, Robert Paul, Barrington Moore, and Herbert Marcuse. *A Critique of Pure Tolerance*. Boston: Beacon Press, 1969.

Chapter 7

Adorno, Theodor W. *Lectures on Negative Dialectics*. Edited by Rolf Tiedemann. Translated by Rodney Livingstone. Cambridge: Polity Press, 2008.

———. *Notes to Literature*. 2 vols. Edited by Rolf Tiedemann. Translated by Shierrby Weber Nicholson. New York: Columbia University Press, 1992.

Adorno, Theodor W., and Walter Benjamin. *The Complete Correspondence 1928–1940*. Edited by Henri Lonitz. Translated by Nicholas Walker. Cambridge, MA: Harvard University Press, 1999.

Buck-Morss, Susan. *The Origins of Negative Dialectics: Theodor W. Adorno, Walter Benjamin, and the Frankfurt Institute.* New York: Free Press, 1979.

Jameson, Fredric. *Late Marxism: Adorno, or, The Persistence of the Dialectic.* London: Verso, 1990.

Jay, Martin. *Adorno.* Cambridge, MA: Harvard University Press, 1984.

Zuidevaart, Lambert. *Adorno's Aesthetic Theory: The Redemption of Illusion.* Cambridge, MA: MIT Press, 1993.

Chapter 8

Adorno, Theodor W. *Introduction to Sociology.* Edited by Christoph Godde. Translated by Edmund Jephcott. Stanford, CA: Stanford University Press, 2000.

———. *Problems of Moral Philosophy.* Edited by Thomas Schröder. Translated by Rodney Livingstone. Stanford, CA: Stanford University Press, 2001.

Adorno, T.W., et al., *The Positivist Dispute in German Sociology.* New York: Harper, 1976.

Berlin, Isaiah. *Against the Current: Essays in the History of Ideas.* Edited by Henry Hardy. New York: Penguin, 1979.

———. *The Magus of the North: J. G. Hamann and the Origins of Modern Irrationalism.* Edited by Henry Hardy. London: John Murray, 1993.

Dumain, Ralph. "The Autodidact Project." Available at http://www.autodidactproject.org/.

Fay, Brian. *Critical Social Science: Liberation and Its Limits.* Ithaca, NY: Cornell University Press, 1987.

Habermas, Jürgen. *Moral Consciousness and Communicative Action.* Translated by Christine Lenhardt and Shierry Weber Nicholson. Cambridge, MA: MIT Press, 1991.

Kirchheimer, Otto. *Politics, Law, and Social Change.* Edited by Frederic S. Burin and Kurt L. Schell. New York: Columbia University Press, 1969.

Marcuse, Herbert. *Technology War and Fascism: Collected Papers,* vol. 1. Edited by Douglas Kellner. New York: Routledge, 1998.

Neumann, Franz. *The Democratic and Authoritarian State.* Edited by Herbert Marcuse. New York: Free Press, 1957.

Further reading

Index